Murder Most Vile
Volume Three
18 Truly Shocking
Murder Cases

Robert Keller

**Please Leave Your Review of This Book At
http://bit.ly/kellerbooks**

ISBN-13: 978-1535195485
ISBN-10: 1535195487

© 2016 by Robert Keller

robertkellerauthor.com

Table of Contents

The Hello Kitty Murder

Hello Kitty is an iconic figure in the Far East. More than a toy, this ubiquitous cat character was created in 1974 by Japan's Sanrio Company, who claim that she weighs as much as "three apples" and likes "small cute things, like stars, candy, and goldfish." She has appeared on over 15,000 products, with more being added all the time. There is even a Hello Kitty amusement Park in Japan.

But in 1999, the famous kitten became associated with something that was everything but cute, the horrific torture murder of a Hong Kong prostitute by a quartet of miscreants who seemed to regard their horrendous acts as no more than an extension of their obsession with video games.

In May of 1999, a pretty 14-year-old girl turned up at the Tsim Sha Tsui police station in Hong Kong. She had a bizarre story to tell. The girl (identified in press coverage of the case only as Melody) said that she was being tormented by the ghost of a woman who she had helped torture to death a year earlier.

Initially skeptical, detectives listened with growing interest as
Melody recounted her tale. She said that she had run away from
home a year earlier, just before the Lunar New Year in 1998.
Hungry, alone and terrified on the streets, she'd wandered into a
cheap restaurant where she'd plopped down in a seat hoping that
someone might take pity on her and buy her a meal.

She'd been sitting there only a short while when a young man slid
into the adjacent booth and struck up a conversation with her. He
said that his name was Leung Wai-lun, although he insisted that
she call him Gangster. He certainly looked the part. In his knocked
off Armani suit, with copious bling, he looked like an extra from an
early Jackie Chan movie. Nonetheless, Melody was besotted. Later
that night, she gave up her virginity to the 18-year-old Leung.

The next months passed in a haze for Melody. She became Leung's
girl and fully embraced his twilight world of love hotels, nightclubs
and karaoke bars.

One night, Leung introduced her to a man named Chan Man-lok, a
ruthless pimp, pornographer, loan shark and drug dealer. Chan
invited Melody and Leung to move into his place, a seven-room
apartment above Kowloon's famous Granville Road shopping
district.

Melody could not help but be impressed by Chan's digs. He had
every amenity she'd ever dreamed of – cable TV, Playstation
games, and an extensive library of Hollywood and Hong Kong
movies. In addition, there was a huge collection of porn, and plenty

of drugs, mainly Ice (Methamphetamine). Chan also appeared to have an obsession with Hello Kitty. His home had Hello Kitty curtains, Hello Kitty bedsheets, and Hello Kitty kitchenware. Scattered about the place were dozens of Hello Kitty dolls, including a mermaid doll which the case would later make infamous.

Melody had been living at the Granville Road apartment for only a couple of weeks when another woman was introduced to the household, a 23-year-old named Fan Man-yee, but known by the street name Ah Map.

Abandoned as a child, Ah Map was raised at Ma Tau Wai girls' home, escaping in her mid-teens to take up a life of drugs, petty crime, and prostitution. In 1997, while working at a Kowloon brothel named the Romance Villa, she met Chan Man-lok, who became a regular client as well as Ah Map's drug supplier. The two often engaged in marathon sex and drug binges together, but after one such session, Ah Map made a fatal mistake, rifling through Chan's wallet after he passed out and stealing $4,000.

It was a stupid crime, with only one possible perpetrator. Chan demanded that Ah Map pay the money back, with interest amounting to an additional $10,000. Yet even after Ah Map complied with these demands, Chan wanted more. He insisted on an additional payment of $16,000. When Ah Map refused, he instructed his accomplices Leung Shing-cho and Leung Wai-lun to kidnap her and bring her to his Granville Road apartment.

The abduction took place on March 17, 1999, whereupon Chan and his henchmen beat Ah Map senseless and told her that she was to remain at the apartment, working as a prostitute and handing over all of her earnings to them, until her debt was paid off.

But their plan had one fatal flaw. They'd beaten Ah Map so badly that she could barely stand, let alone work the streets. And besides, which john was going to pay for at a hooker as battered and bruised as she was?

As it turned out, Chan would never send Ah Map out onto the streets. He and his cohorts were having too much fun beating and torturing her.

Over the weeks that followed, life in the apartment (as described to the police by Melody) picked up a familiar pattern. The three gangsters would get high, play video games, watch movies and torture Ah Map, all the while dreaming up more and more sadistic methods. They burned her with matches and with melted plastic straws, they beat her with sticks and metal pipes, they poured chili sauce into her open wounds and forced her to drink cooking oil. They urinated on her and forced her to eat excrement. On other occasions, they'd string her up from a hook on the ceiling and leave her hanging there overnight. All the while, Ah Map was forced to laugh and smile as she was being brutalized. Failure to do so would result in even more severe punishment.

Melody also participated in the torture and, according to her testimony, she was not an altogether unwilling accomplice. "I did it for fun," she'd later admit. "Just to see what it was like to hurt someone."

No one was ever going to survive the torments heaped on the unfortunate Ah Map for very long. Yet, the young woman lasted for almost a month before eventually succumbing to her injuries. Then, one morning, Melody woke and found Ah Map dead on the bathroom floor, where she'd been left over the previous three days. Her tormentors had apparently become bored of hurting her.

The body remained on the bathroom floor for the next two days, before Chan eventually called his men together and informed them, "She must be destroyed. She will vanish into thin air."

That set in motion a gruesome 10-hour operation to dismember the corpse. Ah Map was lifted into the bathtub, where Chan cut off her head with a wood saw. His accomplices then began slicing flesh from the corpse, bagging it and stashing it in the refrigerator. At one point, Gangster handed Melody a plastic bag stuffed with intestines and told her to cover them with hot water to stop them smelling.

Later, while Leung Shing-cho was cooking the head, he called Melody over and insisted that she look into the pot. "Just pretend you're watching TV," he coaxed.

Melody looked into the pot and saw the head bobbing in the boiling water. "He was right," she later admitted. "It looked like something I saw once in a film."

In the midst of this gory operation, the killers broke for lunch, cooking up a pot of noodles on one plate while the dismembered head was boiling away beside it. They even used the same spoon to stir both pots. Once all of the flesh was boiled from the head, the skull was hidden inside a Hello Kitty mermaid doll where it would remain until the police found it there a year later.

The horrific murder of Ah Map would likely have gone undiscovered had Melody not found herself tormented by the woman's unquiet ghost. As it was, Chan Man-lok, Leung Shing-cho and Leung Wai-lun were arrested and charged with murder. They would eventually be convicted only of manslaughter, the jury deciding that Ah Map's drug use may have contributed to her death. The sentence, though, was the harshest allowed by law. Each of the killers was sentenced to life in prison.

The Family Man

Robert Spangler

At around 10:30 a.m. on December 30, 1978, Timothy Trevithick arrived at the home of his girlfriend Susan Spangler, in Littleton, Colorado. Susan had been expecting him to call that morning, so Timothy found it strange that the door wasn't opened. When his ever more insistent knocking still brought no reply, he walked around the building to the back. That door too was locked, so he let himself in by climbing through a basement window.

The house seemed unnaturally quiet as Timothy climbed the stairs. Reaching the landing he turned left and headed for Susan's bedroom. She was lying face down on her bed, apparently still asleep. It was only when he got closer that he saw the rosette of blood on her back and noticed she wasn't breathing. Timothy backed out of the room, then turned and dashed down the stairs to call the police.

Homicide investigators were soon on the scene and discovered that there were two other victims. Susan's 17-year-old brother

David was in his bedroom, where he lay with his head and shoulders on the floor and his feet on the bed. He'd suffered a single bullet wound to the chest and it appeared that he'd struggled with his killer. The children's mother, Nancy, was found sitting in a chair, slumped over a typewriter where she'd written a suicide note. She'd died of a single shot to the head.

While the police were still processing the scene, the father of the family, Robert Spangler, arrived home. He told the police that he'd been to a movie and wanted to know what had happened. Told of the murders of his family, Spangler seemed oddly calm. He said that he and Nancy had been separated for nine months but that he'd recently moved back in to try and patch things up. Nancy had been suffering from depression, he said, but he'd had no idea she was capable of this.

In any case of spousal murder, the police look first to the surviving partner as the prime suspect. Spangler was questioned and his hands and guns were tested for residue. He agreed to take a polygraph test, saying that he wanted to cooperate in any way that would help bring the perpetrator to book.

But despite Spangler's co-operative stance there were inconsistencies in his testimony, as well as in the evidence left at the scene. For starters, there was no gunpowder on Nancy's hands, while the gloves that Spangler wore showed definite traces of the substance. In order to explain this away, Spangler changed his story. He now claimed that he'd come home and found his family dead. Uncertain of what to do about the situation, he'd gone to a movie to "think things over." Before leaving the house he'd handled the murder weapon and had thus got residue on his gloves.

Implausible though that explanation sounded, the police were unable to prove otherwise. But there were other things about the crime scene that didn't make sense. The shooter had engaged David Spangler in a life and death struggle. Nancy, weighing in at just 100 pounds would have been easily overcome. There was evidence too that the shot that had killed Nancy Spangler had been fired from a distance of eight inches, a most unlikely position for a gunshot suicide. Nancy also suffered from a nervous disorder, which caused her hands to shake. That made it even more improbable that she'd have held the gun at a distance. And the gun was found five and a half feet away from her body.

Lastly, there was testimony that Nancy was devoted to her two children. And there was motive too. Robert Spangler was engaged in a long-term affair with one of his co-workers, Sharon Cooper, despite his claim that he was trying to patch things up with his wife.

In the end, the police had insufficient concrete evidence to charge Spangler. The two polygraphs he submitted to were certainly no help. On each occasion Spangler started hyperventilating, rendering the results useless. He said it was because he was nervous.

Just seven months after the death of his family, Robert Spangler re-married. His new wife was Sharon Cooper, his longtime lover. A fitness fanatic and writer, Sharon loved hiking the Grand Canyon and would later publish a well-received book on the subject. But there was a dark side to Sharon too. She suffered from manic depression and took both prescription and over-the-counter drugs to control her affliction.

In 1986, Robert Spangler paid a visit to Ames, Iowa, to visit his adoptive father. Merlin Spangler was a brilliant scholar and researcher who'd been a professor at Iowa State University. He and his wife Ione had adopted Robert as a baby. Merlin was by now 92, but still active and in excellent health. However, while Robert was visiting, he took a fall and lapsed into a coma. Within two weeks he was dead, leaving a substantial inheritance to his son. Spangler used the windfall to take early retirement.

By 1987, Sharon Spangler's mental health had deteriorated significantly. In December of that year, she made a frantic call to police saying that her husband was "out to get her." Officers summoned to the scene learned that she had fled to a nearby supermarket. They found her hiding in a storeroom, babbling incoherently. She and Spangler divorced soon after.

The divorce settlement hit Spangler hard. He was forced to give up $150,000 from the couple's investments in stocks and bonds, and also to pay $500 per month in spousal support. There was, however, a rather strange clause to the divorce settlement. Should Sharon die before Spangler, he'd be entitled to $20,000 from her estate.

Spangler wasted little time in getting back in the dating game. The ink was barely dry on the divorce papers when he was placing personal ads for a partner. Donna Sundling, a 50-year-old aerobics instructor with five grown children, responded. She soon fell for Robert Spangler's dubious charms. The couple married on August 18, 1990, Donna selling her upmarket condo in Evergreen, Colorado, and moving into Spangler's home in Durango.

Due to the financial setback he'd suffered as a result of his divorce from Sharon, Spangler had had to return to work. But the job he landed suited his outgoing personality to a tee. He became a DJ for country music station KRSJ, where his early morning show gathered a large and loyal following. Meanwhile, he continued to enjoy hiking the Grand Canyon, although he often had to go out on his own. Unlike Sharon, Donna did not enjoy hiking the canyons as she was afraid of heights.

Their differing interests began driving a wedge between Spangler and Donna and it wasn't long before he began thinking about ending his latest marriage. The only thing that stopped him was the thought of the money he'd lose. Divorce was expensive. He'd already found that out the hard way.

Donna must have sensed too that her marriage was in trouble. When Spangler suggested a hiking trip to the Grand Canyon over the Easter weekend in 1993, she agreed. She loved Robert dearly and was more afraid of losing him than she was of facing the canyon's precarious trails.

On Easter Sunday, April 11, 1993, Robert Spangler showed up at the Back Country ranger station. In an oddly calm voice, he told the duty officer that his wife had taken a tragic fall and was lying dead at the bottom of a 160-foot drop at Horseshoe Mesa. He said that they'd stopped there to take a photograph. He'd turned away from her to set up his tripod. When he turned back, Donna was gone. He then looked down into the mesa and saw her broken body lying motionless at the bottom. He scrambled down to help her, but she was already dead. He'd then run to the ranger station to report the tragedy.

A few things bothered the rangers about Spangler's story. For starters, they noted that the spot where Donna fell was the only drop along the entire route that would have resulted in a fatal fall. Second, they found it implausible that Donna would have fallen without crying out. Third, there was Spangler's demeanor. He hardly acted like a man who'd just watched his wife die tragically. Still, suspicion was one thing and proof quite another. Donna Spangler's death was recorded as an accident.

In July 1994, Spangler's second wife Sharon paid him a visit in Durango and ended up staying. Sharon was coming off the back of another failed relationship and was in a fragile state emotionally. Then her beloved dog, Shadow, died, sending her into a deep depression. She spent days locked in her room crying over her loss.

On October 2, 1994, just five months after moving back in with Spangler, 52-year-old Sharon Cooper was dead, her death attributed to an overdose of prescription medication. Spangler, who found the body, told several different versions of events. That was enough to rouse the suspicions of investigators but, as always with Spangler, there was insufficient evidence to press charges. Sharon's death was ruled a suicide.

Unbeknownst to Spangler, events in the background were beginning to move against him. In January 1999, cold case investigators from various jurisdictions met with federal agents in Flagstaff, Arizona. One of the cases that came under discussion was the Spangler murder/suicide. Although officially closed, the case had never been resolved to the satisfaction of Arapahoe County investigators.

After looking over the case files and learning that Robert Spangler had recently been diagnosed with inoperable brain cancer, the Feds recommended that the investigative team should approach Spangler for an interview. They believed that Spangler might be willing to unburden himself, given his terminal condition.

Had Spangler refused to speak to the investigators, the case against him would have died right there. But the Feds decided to appeal to Spangler's ego by telling him that they wanted to interview him because he was such a unique killer. Amazingly it worked. When Spangler arrived the following day, the agents had a file of cardboard boxes stacked outside the door of the interrogation room, all of them labeled "Spangler Task Force." Spangler was seen to give a self-satisfied smile as he noticed them. Once inside, though, he remained cagey, eventually asking for the night to think things over. At that point, the agents were convinced that they'd lost him.

However, Spangler was back the following morning and the interview had barely started when he admitted to killing his first wife, Nancy, and his children, David and Susan. The motive, he said, was so that he could marry Sharon Cooper without the embarrassment and cost of a messy divorce.

The investigative team now had him on three counts of premeditated murder, but Spangler staunchly denied involvement in Sharon Cooper's death. He also refused to discuss the death of his third wife, Donna Sundling, saying that he feared a civil lawsuit by her children.

Again an unorthodox approach loosened Spangler's tongue. The investigators were aware, from talking to Spangler, that he was fascinated with profilers. They hinted that an FBI profiler might be interested in discussing the murders with him, but that they only interviewed serial killers. As Spangler's three murders had been committed in a single incident, he could not be classified as such. Spangler took a moment to mull that over, then grinned and said, "You've got your serial." He then confessed that he'd killed Donna by deliberately pushing her over the 160-foot drop at Horseshoe Mesa.

Robert Spangler would eventually plead guilty to killing Nancy, David, Susan, and Donna. He was sentenced to life imprisonment without parole. He died at the Federal Corrections Medical Center in Springfield, Missouri, on August 5, 2001, ten months after beginning his sentence.

Death in the Valley

Harold Jones

Abertillery is a small town of some 40,000 residents in the south of Wales. Like many towns in the Welsh vales, it prospered during the inter-war years due to the thriving coal mining industry. Most of its men were miners and the camaraderie created by the dangers of working underground made for a strong community spirit. But in 1921, that sense of community was torn apart by the brutal rape-murders of two pre-teen girls. Worse still, the killer was a 15-year-old boy, arrested after the first murder but freed to kill again.

The first murder occurred on the chilly Saturday morning of February 5, 1921. Eight-year-old Freda Burnell had been sent by her father to buy feed for the family's chickens. The feed store was just a short walk away, so when Freda still had not returned after 20 minutes, her father went looking for her. Fred Burnell called first at Mortimer's Corn Stores where the clerk, 15-year-old Harold Jones, confirmed that Freda had indeed visited the store. She'd been his first customer, he said, and had left immediately after making her purchase.

Fred was at first more irritated than concerned. He was convinced that Freda had stopped off to visit one of her friends. After all, Abertillery was a safe town with a close-knit community. He hardly suspected that harm could have come to his little girl. But as he called on all of Freda's friends and then began going door-to-door in search of his daughter, his concern began to grow. Eventually, frantic with worry, he went to the police.

Local officers followed much of the same ground that Fred had, starting with Harold Jones. He repeated his story and insisted that he hadn't seen Freda after she'd left the shop. The police then began knocking on doors and questioning the locals, that too yielding no leads as to the whereabouts of the missing girl. As the light began to fade on that winter day, the police, aided by scores of locals, carried out a search of the town and its adjoining hillsides. Cold and tired, they eventually called off the search at midnight, determined to resume at first light.

At around 7:30 the following morning, one of the searchers came across what he at first thought was a pile of rags, lying on the ground in a lane behind Duke Street. Instead, as he approached, he saw that it was the bloodied corpse of a young girl. Freda had been subjected to a vicious attack. A subsequent autopsy would reveal that she had been raped and then bludgeoned to death. The murder weapon was thought to be an axe. Time of death was put at early the previous day.

As the local constabulary had no experience dealing with this type of crime, Scotland Yard sent a couple of detectives to investigate. They soon honed in on Harold Jones who, as far as anyone could tell, had been the last person to see Freda alive. Jones continued to protest his innocence, but after a witness came forward to claim she'd heard a child's screams coming from Mortimer's Corn Stores on Saturday morning, the police carried out a search of the premises. There they found Freda's handkerchief, as well as an axe that detectives claimed may have been the murder weapon. Harold Jones was then charged with murder.

Jones went on trial at Monmouth Assizes on June 21, 1921. However, the case against him was purely circumstantial and far from watertight. The police had Freda's handkerchief, an axe (which may or may not have been the murder weapon) and a witness who claimed she might have heard a scream. Unsurprisingly, Jones was acquitted.

Few would have anticipated the homecoming that Harold Jones received. The citizens of Abertillery, who had never been convinced that one of their own could have committed such a barbaric crime, put on a parade, complete with a brass band and bunting strung across the streets. Jones was lofted shoulder height and carried through the town. One of those who greeted him most enthusiastically was his neighbor George Little. "Well done son. We knew you didn't do it," Little was heard to say. That remark would soon return to haunt him.

Just seventeen days after Harold Jones' triumphant return to Abertillery, another young girl was missing. 11-year-old Florrie Little was the daughter of the neighbor who had offered Jones such an enthusiastic welcome.

The search, this time, was launched immediately, with Jones among those scouring the streets and countryside for Florrie. He was still thus engaged when the police began conducting house searches, going door-to-door. Harold's father, Phillip, willingly let them into his house and it was there that they found the missing girl, her body stashed in the attic, throat cut and most of the blood drained from the corpse. An autopsy would later prove that she'd also been raped.

As the sensational news of the discovery began filtering through the town, Harold Jones was arrested on the street. This time, there was no denial. He admitted luring Florrie to his house and slashing her throat. He'd then held her over the kitchen sink until she'd bled out. Jones had hoped to get rid of the body but his parents had returned home unexpectedly and he'd been forced to hide the corpse in the attic. A short while later, Florrie's mother had knocked on the door and asked if he'd seen Florrie. Jones had calmly told her that he hadn't seen the girl. He'd then asked her about the wellbeing of her young son, who'd been ill, and wished the boy a speedy recovery.

The timing of Jones' second murder was fortuitous (for him at least). Had he killed Florrie two months later, he would almost certainly have gone to the gallows. As it was, he was two months shy of his sixteenth birthday and therefore ineligible for the death penalty.

On trial at Monmouth again in November 1921, Jones pled guilty to the murder of Florrie Little and also admitted to killing Freda Burnell. He seemed proud of having outwitted the police in the first murder. He said that after attending Freda's funeral, he played a game of billiards then ate a meal and went to bed and slept well. It did not bother him at all. Asked about his motive, Jones said: "A demon had me in his power. A blinding light flashed across my eyes and brain giving the command 'Kill!' – and I did."

Harold Jones was ordered to be detained "at His Majesty's Pleasure." He was held at Wandsworth Prison in London until his eventual release in December 1941, whereupon he promptly disappeared. Unsubstantiated reports have him visiting the sites of his murders in Abertillery in later years. Jones died of cancer in 1971. He is buried in Hammersmith cemetery in West London.

Unthinkable

On a crisp winter morning in 1992, a Chevrolet sedan pulled to the shoulder of a gravel road just outside of Madison, Indiana. Three teenaged girls, dressed in jeans and sweatshirts, exited the vehicle, two of them moving with purpose, the other with what appeared to be reticence. A fourth girl remained in the car. One of the girls, a pretty dark-haired teen, approached the trunk and threw it open. Inside lay the battered body of another girl. Her name was Shanda Sharer and on the last day of her life, January 11, 1992, she was only twelve years old. Her crime? She had become involved in a relationship with the former girlfriend of one of her attackers.

Shanda Sharer was born in Pineville, Kentucky, on June 6, 1979. After her parents divorced, she moved with her mother, Jacqueline Vaught, first to Louisville and later to Jeffersonville, Indiana, where she enrolled at Hazelwood Middle School in June 1991. Shanda was a popular student who was active in volleyball, softball, and cheerleading. However, her mother was less enthused about some of Shanda's other extracurricular activities – specifically her friendship with a fellow student, Amanda Heavrin. Jacqueline suspected that the relationship might be sexual. In an attempt to separate the girls, she moved Shanda to a Catholic school, Our Lady of Perpetual Help, in New Albany.

But Jacqueline Vaught wasn't the only one to take notice of the relationship between Shanda and Amanda. Amanda's ex-lover, Melinda Loveless, was watching too, watching and quietly seething with anger.

Like Shanda Sharer, Melinda Loveless was the product of a broken home. But where Shanda's upbringing had been relatively stable, Melinda's was chaotic, characterized by infidelity and substance abuse on the part of both of her parents, as well as accusations of sexual abuse towards Melinda and her sisters. By her early teens, Melinda was openly gay, something that did not go down well with her mother.

In early 1990, 14-year-old Melinda began dating Amanda Heavrin. However, the relationship was soon in trouble over Melina's obsessive jealousy. By the time Shanda Sharer arrived on the scene, Melinda had moved on and was seeing an older girl. That is, until she heard about Shanda and Amanda. Then she was back, issuing threats of violence, once confronting Shanda in public. When that failed to get the desired result she began thinking about murder, roping her friend Laurie Tackett into the plot.

On the evening of January 10, 1992, 17-year-old Tackett, along with two 15-year-old friends, Toni Lawrence and Hope Rippey, drove from Madison to Melinda Loveless' house in New Albany. Lawrence and Rippey had not previously met Loveless and believed that they were going to attend a rock concert. It was only after arrival at the Loveless home that Melinda showed them a knife and told them that she was going to use it to scare Shanda Sharer. The two girls, who did not know Shanda, readily agreed to the plan.

The foursome drove to Jeffersonville, Indiana, arriving at Shanda's home just before dark. They had discussed their plan on the drive over and decided that Rippey and Lawrence would knock on the door and introduce themselves as friends of Amanda Heavrin. They would tell Shanda that Amanda was waiting to meet her at the "Witch's Castle," a dilapidated stone cottage overlooking the Ohio River, that local teens sometimes used as a make out spot.

But things didn't go quite as planned. Shanda said that she couldn't get out of the house while her mother was awake. She asked them to come back later. The four girls then drove into Louisville where they attended a punk rock concert. When they returned to the house at around 12:30 a.m., Tackett and Rippey went to the door while Lawrence sat behind the wheel and Loveless hid under a blanket in the back seat.

Shanda was told to sit in front. As they drove towards Witch's
Castle, Rippey began questioning her about her relationship with
Amanda Heavrin. Shanda answered these questions freely. In the
back seat, still hidden under the blanket, Loveless listened and
quietly fumed. Eventually, she could stand to hear no more and
sprang from her hiding place, pushing the knife to Shanda's throat.
Now she took over the interrogation, demanding answers from
Shanda about her sexual relationship with Amanda. As their
destination neared, Shanda became increasingly fearful. By the
time they reached Witch's Castle, she was sobbing hysterically.

The girls forced Shanda inside, where they bound her, hand and
foot, with some rope Loveless had brought along for that purpose.
Loveless then began taunting Shanda, threatening to hack off her
hair and removing Shanda's jewelry and handing it out to the
other girls. By now Shanda was crying so uncontrollably that they
feared someone might hear her if they arrived at the cottage. They
therefore took Shanda back to the car and drove off.

While Loveless and Rippey continued taunting Shanda, Tackett
drove them to a local garbage dump. There, Loveless and Tackett
pulled Shanda from the vehicle and ordered her to strip. They then
took turns beating her with a tire iron and after she fell and was
unable to get up, used the same implement to sodomize her.
Finally, they took turns stabbing the fallen girl before strangling
her with a length of rope.

Believing that Shanda was dead, Loveless and Tackett dumped her
body in the trunk of the car and drove towards Tackett's home in
Madison. When they arrived, they went inside to clean themselves
up. They'd barely begun when Shanda regained consciousness and

began screaming and thumping on the inside of the trunk. Afraid that the screams might wake her mother, Tackett grabbed a paring knife and ran out to the car. She returned a few minutes later, covered in blood and told the others that she had stabbed Shanda to death.

It was now 2:30 a.m. and the girls had to start thinking about disposing of their victim's body. It was decided that Tackett and Loveless would do the job while Lawrence and Rippey stayed behind. Yet despite the horrendous torture meted out on her, Shanda was still not dead. She again began screaming, whereupon Tackett pulled over, opened the trunk and beat her unconscious with the tire iron.

Loveless and Tackett arrived back at Tackett's house just before daybreak. After picking up Rippey and Lawrence, they stopped at a gas station in Madison to fill a two-liter Pepsi bottle with gasoline. Then they drove to a remote area off U.S. Route 421, where Tackett and Rippey wrapped Shanda in a blanket and carried her into a field. Loveless accompanied them, while Lawrence, perhaps now realizing the implications of what they were about to do, refused to participate and remained in the car. A few moments after her friends walked into the field, Lawrence saw a lick of flame and smelled seared flesh. An autopsy would later reveal that Shanda Sharer was still alive when she was set alight.

Shanda's body did not lay undiscovered for long. That same morning, hunters chanced upon the gruesome remains and called the police. And it did not take long for the police to identify the victim, or the perpetrators. Just after 8 o'clock that evening, a hysterical Toni Lawrence arrived at the Jefferson County Sheriff's office, accompanied by her parents. She gave a rambling statement, describing the horrendous murder, identifying the victim as "Shanda," and naming the three other girls involved. Shanda had by now been reported missing by her mother, so the pieces came together quickly after that.

Loveless, Tackett and Rippey were arrested on January 12, with the Jefferson County prosecutor declaring his intention to try all four girls as adults. Faced with the very real prospect of the death penalty, the four accused quickly asked for a deal.

In terms of those deals, Laurie Tackett and Melinda Loveless were sentenced to 60 years in the Indiana Women's Prison in Indianapolis. With time off for good behavior, they could walk free in 2022, when both will be in their mid-forties. Hope Rippey was sentenced to 60 years and was released on April 28, 2006, having served just 14. Toni Lawrence, who did not directly participate in the murder, served nine years and was released in December 2000.

Slayer's Book of Death

Jason Massey

On the morning of July 29, 1993, a maintenance crew was working along a stretch of Cutoff Road in Ellis County, Texas. It was a mid-summer day and the workers were suffering in the stifling heat. As one of them took a break from his labors, he spotted something pale lying in the undergrowth beside a nearby creek. The man alerted another worker and the two of them scaled the low, barbed wire fence and made their way through the brush to where the object lay. As they approached, they picked up the unmistakable stench of decomposition and to their horror realized that the object was a naked corpse, partially obscured by brush. While one remained to guard the scene, the other raced to the nearby town of Telico to notify the police. Neither of them noticed that the body had been severely mutilated and was missing its head and hands.

Police officers determined that the corpse was of a young female. Then, as they fanned out across the area looking for clues, they made another shocking discovery. A second body lay some three hundred yards from the first. This one was a male, no older than his mid-teens. Unlike the female victim, he was fully clothed and had not been mutilated. He'd died from a bullet wound to the back of the head.

The police soon identified the male victim. In his pocket was a wallet with a library card in the name "James B. King." The card had been issued in the nearby town of Terrell and when the police checked on missing person's reports from that jurisdiction, they picked up the name of Brian King, a 14-year old reported missing three days earlier. Also missing was his 13-year-old stepsister, Christina Benjamin. DNA matching would soon confirm that the headless corpse was Christina.

Investigators meanwhile went to question James King, the children's father. He told them a strange tale about the night they'd disappeared. He'd been awakened at around midnight, he said, by the sound of a car horn. Going to the front door, he'd peered out into the street and seen Brian (who had been sleeping on the porch) talking to the driver of a tan car of Japanese make. He'd also spotted someone in the back seat of the vehicle, someone with long blond hair. Figuring that these were probably friends of Brian's, he decided to give his son five minutes before calling him inside. In the meanwhile, he went to use the bathroom. When he returned, both the car and Brian were gone.

James King waited an hour for Brian to return. When he did not, James returned to bed, determined to give his son a talking to, for sneaking off in the middle of the night. But Brian had not returned home by the following morning and there was an even more disconcerting discovery. His sister Christine was also missing. After frantic calls to family and friends turned up no trace of the missing teens, James and his wife carried out a search of the neighborhood. Then James called the police.

The police now had back the autopsy report on Christina Benjamin, and the sheer ferocity of the attack left them in no doubt that they urgently needed to catch the perpetrator. He was very likely to kill again.

Christina had died from a .22 bullet to the back. Her head and hands had then been severed, with either a hunting knife or an axe. However, the horrific mutilations did not stop there. There were extensive cuts on the abdomen, thighs, and genital area and a deep incision had been made to her stomach, giving the killer access to the internal organs. He'd used that access to inflict horrendous injuries on the liver and to pull out her intestines. Both of the victim's nipples were also sliced off and were missing from the scene.

The police also lifted some important forensic evidence, including a long blond hair found on Brian King's jeans and believed to be from the killer, and carpet fibers, which were determined to be from a tan vehicle of Japanese make. None of the evidence, though, would be any good unless they had a suspect to match it to. That suspect was soon forthcoming. An anonymous caller offered up the name Jason Massey. Massey, he said, had a history of killing and mutilating animals, often spoke of his admiration for Charles Manson, and liked to talk about his plans for abducting, killing and mutilating young girls.

As the police began investigating Massey's background, he began to look more and more like a viable suspect. The 20-year-old high school dropout had a record for petty theft, stalking, and animal abuse. He'd been suspected of killing and mutilating the pet dog of a girl who'd refused to go out with him. On another occasion, officers had pulled him over for a suspected DUI and found a strangled cat in his vehicle. Aside from this, Massey drove a tan Subaru and he had long, blond hair, like the man in the backseat of the car that had picked up Brian, like the hair found on Brian's jeans. Massey was pulled in for questioning, then arrested and charged with capital murder. Now the police had to build a case against him.

A search of Massey's residence produced a plethora of circumstantial evidence, newspaper clippings, items of female clothing and a pair of handcuffs with traces of blood on them. There was also a stash of pornography, and books on Satanism and police procedure. Massey's Subaru yielded more evidence. The car had obviously been given a thorough cleaning recently but investigators were still able to find traces of blood in the vehicle and also on a knife and hammer. The police also took carpet fibers from the Subaru, for comparison to the fibers found on Brian King. Lab results provided a match. The blood found in the vehicle and on the weapons would be matched to Christina Benjamin and the blond hair found on Brian King would be positively matched to Massey. It all made for a strong circumstantial case.

But County Prosecutor Clay Strange was worried. There had been a second man in the car on the night of the murder and despite their efforts the police had been unable to find him. A sharp defense attorney would no doubt seize on that and challenge the prosecution to prove that it was his client, rather than this second man, who had committed the murders. It might just be enough to create a reasonable doubt. When the matter came to trial in September 1994, that was exactly the line of reasoning the defense followed.

Massey might well have walked on the murder charges had it not been for a chance discovery made while the trial was in progress. A hiker walking through some woods came across a scuffed red cooler box. Opening it, he was shocked to discover the skulls of several dozen animals. Among this carnage, wrapped in plastic, were four spiral notebooks, labeled "The Slayer's Book of Death Volumes 1-4, the thoughts of Jason Massey." The hiker, who had been following the case, knew that this was potentially important evidence, and so handed it over to the police.

The notebooks were filled cover to cover with handwritten journal entries starting in 1989 and ending just after the murders of Brian King and Christina Benjamin. In them, Massey describes his various acts of depravity against animals, including the killing of the dog whose owner had refused to date him. He goes on to state his greatest ambition, to become America's most infamous serial killer. "My goal is to kill 700 people in twenty years," he wrote. Perhaps more importantly, he expressed his desire to kill and mutilate a young girl, the mutilations he described matching those inflicted on Christina almost exactly.

On October 6, 1994, the jury took just three hours to convict Jason Massey of murder. On October 12, 1994, they voted for the death penalty.

Jason Massey was sent to Death Row in Huntsville, Texas, to await execution. First, though, there was the lengthy appeals procedure to be navigated, a process that took up the next six years and ultimately failed.

On the evening of April 3, 2001, Massey was strapped to a gurney and wheeled into the death chamber at Huntsville. Before his execution, he eventually came clean and admitted to killing Brian and Christina. Looking directly at the King family, he said:

"I do not know any of y'all and that is unfortunate because I would like to apologize to each and every one of you individually. I can't imagine what I've taken from you. I want you to know I did do it. I'm sorry for what I have done. I want you to know that Christina did not suffer as much as you think she did. I know you guys want to know where the rest of her remains are. I put her remains in the Trinity River."

As the lethal cocktail of drugs began to flow, Massey recited a biblical verse. Moments later he let out a gasp and lay still. He was pronounced dead at 6:20 p.m. Jason Massey was twenty-eight years old at the time of his death. His demise was far more merciful than those he'd granted his victims.

The Bath Massacre

School massacres occur with tragic regularity in the United States, the most infamous perhaps the outrage committed by Eric Harris and Dylan Klebold at Columbine High School on April 20, 1999. But long before Harris and Klebold (or even their parents) were born, an event occurred that was far more deadly than Columbine. It happened in Bath, Michigan, on May 18, 1927. The perpetrator was a disgruntled school board administrator named Andrew Kehoe.

Andrew Kehoe was born in Tecumseh, Michigan, on February 1, 1872, one of thirteen children. His mother died when Andrew was still a boy and his father soon remarried. Andrew disliked his stepmother and the two of them often clashed. When Kehoe was fourteen, a tragedy occurred in the household. While his stepmother was attempting to light an oil stove, the contraption exploded, coating her in burning flames. Kehoe, who was present, reportedly made no effort to help the burning woman as she writhed in agony. She died of her injuries a few days later. The local authorities suspected that the stove had been tampered with but were unable to prove it and the investigation went no further.

A few years after his stepmother's death, Andrew Kehoe graduated from Tecumseh High School and was accepted into Michigan State University. It was while studying at MSU that he met his future wife, Ellen "Nellie" Price. Ellen was quite a catch for Kehoe, the daughter of a wealthy Lansing family. The couple wed in 1912 and spent the first seven years of their marriage drifting from place to place before Kehoe decided he wanted to become a farmer. $6,000 in cash and a $6,000 mortgage secured them a 185-acre spread outside the village of Bath, Michigan, and the Kehoe's settled down to the agricultural life.

However, it was soon clear to the local community that Andrew Kehoe was no farmer. A meticulous man, who was known to change his clothing several times a day, Kehoe preferred tinkering with machinery to actual farm work. According to neighbors he was always trying to come up with better and easier ways of doing things, rather than following tried and tested methods. He was also known to have a short fuse and to treat his farm animals poorly. He once beat a horse to death in a fit of temper.

Despite these shortcomings, Kehoe was regarded as an intelligent man, and his reputation for thriftiness saw him elected treasurer of the Bath Consolidated School board in 1924. In 1925, Kehoe was appointed Bath Township Clerk, although he lost the position in the subsequent year's election. By then he was already in financial dire straits, a situation exacerbated by his wife Nellie contracting tuberculosis.

Around this time the usually argumentative Kehoe became ever more combative. At school board meetings, he repeatedly accused superintendent Emory Huyck of financial mismanagement. He also rallied against a local property tax, imposed to finance the building and maintenance of the consolidated school. Kehoe blamed this tax for all of his woes when in reality a combination of poor farm management, unnecessary purchases of expensive farm equipment, and his wife's medical bills lay at the root of his problems. By 1927, Kehoe had stopped making mortgage payments and the bank was getting ready to foreclose on his property. Seething with anger, Kehoe began planning a horrendous revenge.

In order to make sense of Kehoe's subsequent actions, it is necessary to have a cursory understanding of the school system of the era. Many schools at that time were still simple one-room affairs where children of different ages shared the same classroom and teacher. In 1922, the citizens of Bath voted for the formation of the Bath Consolidated School, incorporating the various rural schools in the area. Construction of the school was completed in 1923, funded by the increased property taxes that lay at the root of Kehoe's grievance. At the time of the Bath disaster, there were 236 students enrolled, ranging from the first to twelfth grades.

In the winter of 1926, Kehoe volunteered to perform maintenance around the school. Kehoe was known locally as a talented handyman and as the move would save money, the school board readily agreed. No one could have known that it was a ruse by Kehoe to be allowed access to the school basement at any time without raising suspicion.

At around that time, Kehoe began building up a stock of pyrotol, an explosive invented during World War I. Farmers often used the substance to clear boulders and tree stumps from their fields, so Kehoe's purchases, amounting to almost a ton of the incendiary, raised no alarm. Neither did his order of two boxes of dynamite from a local sporting goods store. Over the months that followed, Kehoe carried quantities of pyrotol and dynamite into the basement of the school building and began rigging his charges. Eventually, on May 18, 1927, he was ready to act.

At around 8:45 on that bright spring morning, neighbors noticed smoke coming from the direction of the Kehoe farmhouse. One of them phoned the fire department and firefighters were dispatched to the area. Meanwhile, Andrew Kehoe was at the school. Witnesses saw him enter the building at around 9:15 and later run from the premises, get into his truck and race off. Not long after, the firefighters, closing on the Keogh farm, heard a massive explosion from the direction of Bath. They immediately abandoned their mission and raced towards town.

Kehoe had detonated his explosives under the north wing of the building at 9:45, causing the walls to collapse and the roof to cave in. First-grade teacher Bernice Sterling later recalled that the effect of the explosion was similar to a massive earthquake. "It seemed as though the floor went up several feet," she said. "After the first shock, I thought for a moment I was blind. The air seemed to be full of children and flying desks and books. Children were tossed high in the air. Some were catapulted out of the building."

As the dust began to settle, the full extent of the horror became clear. Protruding from the rubble were the broken, blood-spattered, bodies of dead children, many of them as young as five or six. Distraught parents who had by now reached the school, tried in vain to lift the collapsed roof. Eventually one of them, Monty Ellsworth, decided to drive back to his farm in order to fetch a heavy rope. On route, he passed Andrew Kehoe, driving back towards the school in his pickup. Kehoe, Ellsworth would later testify, was grinning from ear to ear.

Meanwhile, chaos reigned at the Bath School, with desperate parents clawing through the ruins, calling out the names of their children. Soon a row of tiny bodies was arrayed on the school lawn with mothers sobbing and clutching the destroyed corpses of their children. With all of this going on, nobody took much notice as Andrew Kehoe's pickup slid back into the school parking lot.

Kehoe scoured the chaos and spotted Superintendent Huyck, so often his nemesis. He summoned Huyck towards him. Then, as Huyck approached Kehoe picked up a rifle, turned in his seat and fired a single shot into the cab. In the next moment, a second explosion rocked Bath. The pickup, packed with dynamite and shrapnel, was entirely destroyed, killing Kehoe and Huyck instantly. Bath postmaster Glenn O. Smith, and Nelson McFarren, a retired farmer were also killed, as was Cleo Claton, an eight-year-old who had just staggered from the collapsed school building.

As the dust settled after the second explosion, rescue workers and ordinary citizens moved in to search for survivors, disregarding their own safety. Firefighters, police officers, and medical staff streamed in from nearby towns to help. The dead were removed to the city hall while the town pharmacy became a makeshift triage center. A local bakery provided free food and drink to the rescuers. Meanwhile, the injured and dying were transported to Sparrow Hospital and to St. Lawrence Hospital in Lansing. In the midst of it all, the fire department found 500 pounds of undetonated explosives, rigged to a timer, in the school basement. Kehoe's second charge, which would have destroyed the south wing of the school building, had failed to detonate.

Police and fire officials had also been dispatched to the Kehoe property where they found the farmhouse a smoldering ruin. The following day, investigators found Nellie Kehoe, her body burned beyond recognition. An autopsy would later determine that she had been bludgeoned to death before being set alight. As a final cruelty, Kehoe had penned all of his farm animals in the barn. The animals had been burned alive.

Kehoe had left one final message to the authorities. On a wooden board, he'd neatly stenciled in large black letters, "CRIMINALS ARE MADE, NOT BORN."

Forty-four people died as a result of Andrew Kehoe's deadly actions, 38 of them children. It remains to this day, America's worst school massacre.

Celine's Last Ride

In December 1995, Celine Figard set off from her home near the French-Swiss border to travel across Europe. The 19-year-old accountancy student had been offered a holiday job at the Ashburn Hotel in Fordingbridge, England. She'd worked at the hotel the previous year and had enjoyed her time there, so when the chance came up, she jumped at it.

Celine's parents were less enamored with the idea, especially as a transport strike meant that Celine would have to hitchhike across France. Although Celine was a sensible girl with a good head on her shoulders, they were acutely aware that their pretty daughter was overly trusting of people. Their fears were somewhat allayed when the son of a family friend, a truck driver, offered to drive Celine to England where he was contracted to make a delivery. The pair set off in early December 1995.

One of the stops Celine and her chaperone made was at the vineyard of Pascal Chretien, who was so impressed with the attractive young lady that he presented her with two bottles of his vintage champagne. Celine intended taking these with her to England, to share with her friends over Christmas.

Celine's friend drove her as far as a truck stop in Ashford, Kent, where he arranged for another French driver, Roger Bouvier, to take her onward. Bouvier was able to drive her to a service area near Newbury, Berkshire. From there, Celine intended hitching another ride, to complete the last leg of her 500-mile journey. Bouvier tried to warn her against doing so, suggesting that she complete her journey by bus, but Celine laughed it off, insisting that she'd be fine. As Bouvier watched, she approached the driver of a white Mercedes truck. As she left with the driver, she leaned out of the window and shouted a cheerful Christmas greeting to Bouvier. It would be a Christmas that Celine Figard never got to celebrate.

Celine was expected at the Ashburn Hotel on December 20. When she failed to show, the hotel owners were not too concerned. They assumed that she'd been delayed by the French transport strike. However, when another day passed and there was still no word from Celine, they phoned her parents. Bernard and Martine Figard immediately sensed that something was wrong. They asked hotel staff to report the matter to the police.

The report landed on the desk of Detective Chief Superintendent John McGammont who from the start suspected that this was more than a missing person case. After tracing the two French drivers Celine had traveled with, McGammont learned of the white Mercedes truck and ordered his men to track down the drivers of all 7,500 such units registered in Britain and question them. It was a mammoth task. While that was ongoing, McGammont distributed Celine's photograph and description to the media, in the hope that someone might have seen her.

A month passed with no break in the case. In the meanwhile, the police had sent out more than 25,000 letters to registered truck drivers, requesting their help. One of those went to a stocky 37-year-old from Poole in Dorset, named Stuart Morgan. Morgan drove a white Mercedes tractor, which he sometimes parked on the forecourt of a service station opposite his home. As a gesture of thanks that Christmas, he'd presented the owners of the service station with two bottles of vintage French champagne.

December 29 brought the tragic turn in the case that police had long expected. Celine Figard's naked, battered body was found by a motorist alongside the A499 freeway near Worcester. She had been raped, beaten and strangled.

The day after Celine was found, the police questioned Stuart Morgan, as part of their operation to interview all drivers of white Mercedes units. Morgan denied knowing Celine and insisted that he'd been nowhere near the truck stop where she'd last been seen alive. He even produced the tachographs from his vehicle, to support his story. The police then asked Morgan to submit a DNA sample for comparison against semen lifted from the victim. Morgan refused, immediately elevating him to the top of the suspect list. The police soon learned that his tachograph had been falsified and that cell phone records placed him definitely in the area of Newbury on the date of Celine's disappearance.

The police now had enough evidence to bring Morgan in, but they held back, hoping to strengthen their case. In the interim, they ran background checks on their quarry and found that he was a twice-married man who was the father of twin girls and an 11-year-old son. Morgan had no previous convictions, although he had been questioned by police regarding his involvement in a smuggling ring that brought alcohol and cigarettes into the UK. Those who knew him said that he had a short temper and that he was a serial philanderer who enjoyed bragging about his exploits with female hitchhikers.

The final piece of evidence linking Morgan to Celine's disappearance fell into place when the police learned of the two bottles of champagne Morgan had given to the service station owners. Those bottles proved to be the same ones presented to Celine by Pascal Chretien.

Morgan was arrested on February 17, 1996. A search of his home firmed up the case against him, uncovering Celine Figard's rucksack, complete with her personal photographs and identification documents. The police also found the lower bunk from Morgan's truck, still damp with blood. DNA testing would prove that the blood was Celine's.

Faced with the evidence against him Morgan changed his story. He now admitted that he'd given Celine a ride and also confessed that he'd had sex with her. However, the sex, according to Morgan, had been consensual and indeed, had been initiated by Celine. She had been alive and well when he'd dropped her off, he insisted. The story was ludicrous and given short shrift by the police. On February 21, Stuart Morgan was charged with murder.

Morgan's trial began at Worcester Crown Court on October 2, 1996. He entered a plea of not guilty and listened impassively as the prosecutor outlined the horrendous end to Celine Figard's short life. Shortly after picking up Celine, Morgan had manufactured some excuse to pull into a lay-by where he'd beaten Celine into submission before binding her hands with adhesive tape and raping her. He'd then strangled the girl, stowed her body on the lower bunk of his sleeper cab and continued on to Southampton, where he'd picked up a container for delivery to Bradford, in the north of England. Over the next 10 days, Celine's body had lain in the cab until the stench of putrefaction had become too much and Morgan had been forced to dump it. During that time, Morgan had slept on the upper bunk, with the decomposing corpse on the bunk below him.

Responding to the prosecution case, Morgan took the stand in his own defense. He repeated his ludicrous tale that Celine had willingly engaged in sex within an hour of meeting him, something that Celine's family and friends insisted would have been entirely out of character. He stuck to his story of having released Celine unharmed but could not explain her blood in his truck, nor her rucksack in his possession. Asked why he hadn't come forward when Celine's disappearance was made public, Morgan said that he'd been afraid his story would not be believed. He was right in that assumption.

On October 16, the jury unanimously found Stuart Morgan guilty of murder. The judge then sentenced him to life imprisonment. In the wake of Morgan's conviction, there was media speculation that he might be the "Midlands Ripper," an as yet unidentified serial killer, responsible for the deaths of several women raped and murdered along various highways. Senior police officers refused to comment.

Weeds

Herbert Rowse Armstrong was born in 1870 at Newton Abbot, Devon. He was a bright boy who excelled at his studies and was accepted into Cambridge University after finishing school. There he studied law, becoming a solicitor in 1895. Armstrong initially practiced law in his hometown of Newton Abbott before moving to Liverpool. He later became a partner at a legal firm in the small town of Hay-on-Wye on the Welsh/English border.

Armstrong's improved circumstances allowed him to propose to Katherine Mary Friend, who he knew from Newton Abbot. The couple married in 1907, setting up home in the village of Cusop Dingle. They had three children in as many years, before moving into a bigger house, also in Cusop, in 1910. There, Armstrong developed an interest in gardening. He appeared to have an obsession with eradicating weeds and was known to mix up his own weed-killing concoctions, many of them containing arsenic.

The Armstrongs were doing well. Herbert's legal practice was thriving, while Katherine was financially independent with an income of her own. Herbert's only annoyance was a rival legal firm in the small town, operated by an elderly solicitor named Griffiths.

After the outbreak of World War I in August 1914, Armstrong was called up to the army with the rank of captain. He was later promoted to major and posted to France. A few months later, he was allowed to return to England so that he could look after his legal practice. From then on, Armstrong insisted on being addressed by his military rank.

By the time Armstrong was discharged from the military in 1919, his rival Griffiths was frail and sickly. Armstrong saw an opportunity to move in on his practice and proposed a merger but Griffiths turned him down. Instead, he brought in a younger partner, Oswald Norman Martin. When Griffiths died in 1920, Martin took over the practice.

With the war over, life returned to normal in Cusop Dingle. For Armstrong, that meant that he went from being a military officer to being a henpecked husband. The diminutive major stood just over 5 foot tall and weighed no more than 100 pounds. Mrs. Armstrong, although not much taller, dominated him in every respect. She treated him more like one of her children than like a husband. Armstrong was only allowed to smoke in one room of the house and never in public. He was not allowed to drink alcohol. His wife often berated and humiliated him in company. On more than one occasion she called him away from a meeting at his practice and ordered him home because it was his bath night. Although Mrs. Armstrong was well respected in the town, many residents had sympathy for the Major.

From around May 1920, Major Armstrong began making periodic visits to London, ostensibly on business, although it would later emerge that he had dinner with a lady friend on several occasions. In July 1920, Armstrong drew up a new will for his wife, in which she left everything to him. Around the time, he also took up his weed-killing exploits with new vigor, making several purchases of arsenic.

During August 1920, Mrs. Armstrong became ill. She also began having hallucinations and visions, her mental health deteriorating to such an extent that she was declared insane and committed to the Barnwood Asylum in Gloucester. Early in January, Armstrong petitioned to have Katherine returned to his care. Before her homecoming on January 22, 1921, he purchased a quarter pound of arsenic from the local chemist shop. A month later, Katherine Armstrong was dead.

Katherine's death was attributed to a combination of heart disease and gastritis. She was buried in the churchyard at Cusop, her husband suffering his loss with admirable dignity. In his diary would later be found a terse entry, "K died."

Following Mrs. Armstrong's death, the residents of Cusop noticed a change in Major Armstrong. Relieved of the shackles imposed by his wife, the once-timid major became much more assertive, more outgoing. He began making regular visits to London, while in his home village he aggressively chased business, even pursuing established clients of his rival, Mr. Martin. At the same time, Martin was pressing him to pay an outstanding sum of £500, required to conclude a property deal for which Martin was acting as notary. Armstrong, who had inherited over £2,000 from his wife's estate, could easily have afforded the amount, but he seemed to take a perverse pleasure in keeping Martin waiting.

Shortly after Katherine Armstrong's death, Martin received a box of chocolates, delivered to his house anonymously. Assuming they'd been sent by an appreciative client, he passed them on to his wife. She offered them to guests at a dinner party, one of whom became violently ill after sampling the candy. The chocolates were sent to a toxicologist who found that they had been infused with arsenic. Martin was baffled as to who might have tried to poison him.

On October 26, 1921, Armstrong invited Martin to his home to take tea and eventually conclude the outstanding property deal. During tea, Armstrong reached for a buttered scone and passed it to Martin, saying, "Excuse my fingers." Martin ate the scone, and later that evening, after returning home, he was violently ill.

Dr. Thomas Hincks, who had attended Mrs. Armstrong, was called. He found Martin in bed, extremely bilious and with a rapid pulse. The elevated pulse rate seemed at odds with the doctor's original impression that Martin might be suffering from a stomach bug, so he took a urine sample and sent it for analysis. A week later, the results were in. Martin had ingested arsenic.

After eliminating all other possible sources of the poison, the doctor reached the conclusion that Martin had been deliberately poisoned. As no one else in the Martin household was suffering similar symptoms, it could be safely deduced that the poison had been administered outside the home and after questioning Martin, the doctor learned of the meal he'd had at Armstrong's house. Hincks then decided to inform the Home Office in London. As he had no proof of wrongdoing he did not involve the local constabulary, although he did share his concerns with Martin.

The authorities eventually decided to take action in December, dispatching Chief Inspector Crutchett to look into the matter. He conducted discreet inquiries, not wanting to alert Armstrong until there was sufficient evidence to charge him. In the interim, Armstrong made several attempts to invite Martin and his wife to tea. Each time, Martin politely declined.

On December 31, Crutchett eventually felt he had enough evidence to charge Armstrong with attempted murder. Two days later, an exhumation order was obtained for Mrs. Armstrong, the famed pathologist Bernard Spilsbury carrying out the examination and finding copious amounts of arsenic in her system. On January 19, Armstrong was charged with the murder of his wife.

Armstrong went on trial at Hereford Assizes on April 3, 1922. His defense was based on the theory that Mrs. Armstrong was mentally ill and had committed suicide by ingesting the arsenic. However, this did not tally with the evidence. The defense provided proof that Katherine Armstrong had been bed-ridden during the last week of her life and therefore incapable of walking to the shed where the poison was stored. Her nurse also testified that Katherine had been fearful of dying and had told her on the morning of the day she died: "I have everything to live for - my children and my husband."

This evidence was compelling but perhaps even more damaging to Armstrong was testimony that he was afflicted with syphilis. This countered the impression the defense was trying to present of Armstrong as a professional, god-fearing man, wrongly accused. In the end, it took the jury just 14 minutes to convict him.

Armstrong was sentenced to hang and after the Court of Appeal turned down his petition he was duly executed at Gloucester Prison on May 31, 1922. He maintained his innocence to the end but to his credit, he went to his death without complaint. Armstrong's nemesis, Oswald Martin, lived only two years longer. Afflicted by nightmares after the attempt on his life, he fell into a deep depression. His health failed and he died in 1924.

Voodoo Lady

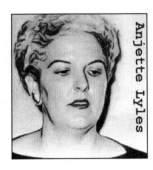

Anjette Donovan Lyles was born in Macon, Georgia, on August 23, 1925, the only daughter of Jetta Watkins and William Donovan. She grew up to be a pretty girl with a charming personality, which she used to good effect. The young Anjette was said to have a remarkable skill for bending people to her will and getting her own way.

In October 1947, the 22-year-old Anjette married Ben Lyles, whose family owned the popular Lyles Restaurant in downtown Macon. The marriage would be blessed with two daughters, Marcia, born 1948, and Carla, born in 1951. During this time, Anjette was assisting her in-laws in running the restaurant and showed a natural aptitude for the job, proving a big hit with customers.

Unfortunately, the same could not be said for her husband, Ben. He was a heavy drinker, prone to staying out late at night, drinking, gambling and tomcatting. On the surface, Anjette appeared to accept his indiscretions without complaint. However, she found it hard to hide her anger when he sold the restaurant for just $2,500 to settle his gambling debts.

Lyle did not live long after that. Just six months later, in December 1951, his health rapidly deteriorated. He began bleeding profusely from his nose and mouth, his legs and arms swelled and his body at times became extremely rigid, with convulsive twitching of the limbs. Eventually, he lapsed into a coma and died at Macon Hospital on January 25, 1952, his death attributed to encephalitis.

Widowed at the age of 26, and with two young children to support, Anjette was forced to accept charity from her family in the form of money and used clothes for her daughters. However, Anjette was nothing if not determined. She soon found employment as a bookkeeper at the Bell House Restaurant. The job served a dual purpose. It provided her with money to support her young family and allowed her to learn the restaurant business from the ground up. Anjette had already determined that she wanted to buy back Lyles' and in April 1955, after years of scrimping and saving, she did just that, paying $12,000 for the restaurant and reopening it as Anjette's.

The restaurant was a hit from the start and was soon the most popular eatery in Macon. The traditional southern cuisine it served was good, although not spectacular. The key to its success lay in the sparkling personality of its proprietress. Anjette greeted her customers at the door with a hug and took the time to stop by at each table for a chat. Her good looks and flirtatious manner made the venue particularly popular with Macon's leading male citizens, including judges, lawyers, businessmen and civic leaders. Lyles was linked romantically with several men in the community, but there was nothing to substantiate the rumors.

In 1955, Anjette began seeing Joe Neal "Buddy" Gabbert, a commercial airline pilot and military veteran. The couple married in Carlsbad, New Mexico, in June of that year.

Four months after they returned to Macon, Buddy began complaining of pain in his wrist. Shortly thereafter, he developed a severe rash, which covered his face, chest, arms, and legs. His legs and arms also swelled acutely, causing such pain that he begged to be allowed to die. Anjette, meanwhile, appeared distraught. "I know he's going to die," she confided in acquaintances.

Eventually, Buddy's condition became so severe that he was hospitalized. A few days in the hospital and he'd recovered enough to be returned to his wife's care. However, his condition soon worsened again. He was unable to eat but was nonetheless racked by bouts of painful vomiting. Admitted to the VA hospital in Dublin, Georgia, Buddy held on until December 2, when he died of kidney failure.

The doctors who had attended Buddy wanted to carry out an autopsy, but Anjette stoutly refused. "I promised him I'd never let anyone cut him up," she insisted. The doctors carried out the autopsy anyway but found nothing untoward.

In the wake of Buddy's death, Anjette hardly behaved like a grieving widow. She cashed in his life insurance policy, bought herself a new Cadillac and was soon dating Buddy's former boss,

Bob Franks. She also bought herself a new home in the suburbs
and invited her former mother-in-law, Julia Lyles, to live with her.
This had less to do with charity than Anjette's knowledge that Julia
had nearly $100,000 in savings. Julia had barely moved in before
Anjette was pressuring her into making a will.

In August 1957, Julia took ill. She was listless and pale and despite
the heat of a Georgia summer, complained of feeling cold. As her
condition worsened, she began vomiting blood and her limbs
swelled up and took on an unearthly purple hue. After Julia was
hospitalized, Anjette continued to visit her, usually bringing her
favorite foods from the restaurant and earning admiration from all
quarters for her devotion. Meanwhile, Julia's condition continued
to deteriorate and Anjette followed her familiar pattern of
confiding in acquaintances that Julia wasn't going to make it.

In late September Anjette showed friends a note, ostensibly from
Julia, asking her to make funeral arrangements. On September 29,
Julia Lyles was dead. A week later Anjette produced Julia's will.
One-third of the estate went to Julia's son Joseph, one-third to
Anjette, and the final portion to Anjette's daughters, Marcia and
Carla. As Anjette was the trustee for the girls, she had effectively
gained $66,000 from Julia's death.

Anjette had always been a deeply superstitious woman, and at
some point, she became involved in voodoo. She consulted
fortunetellers and witchdoctors and even tried to cast her own
spells. Her restaurant staff would often find her burning candles of
various colors in the kitchen and speaking to the flames. When
asked, she readily explained her activities. "If you desire a certain

result, you write it on a note and place it under a lit candle," she said. "You tell it what you want it to do."

But Anjette's voodoo spells appeared powerless to stop those around her coming to harm. In March 1958, her older daughter, 9-year-old Marcia, developed a bad cough. When her temperature suddenly rocketed to 106 degrees, her doctor ordered her hospitalized. Anjette, as was her wont, began immediately predicting her daughter's death.

Shortly after Marcia fell ill, Julia Lyles' sister, Nora Bagley, received an anonymous note, which suggested that Marcia had been poisoned. She passed the note on to the authorities but before they had a chance to investigate, Marcia's health rapidly deteriorated. She became delirious and started screaming about bugs and snakes crawling on her skin. She died on April 4, 1958.

Marcia was buried in the family plot at Coleman Chapel near Wadley, in eastern Georgia. Her mother placed a Bible and a bride doll in the little girl's coffin and at the funeral made an ominous remark. "Carla says she wants to go to heaven to be with Marcia," she told mourners.

But Anjette's days as a serial killer were rapidly drawing to a close. Based on the anonymous tip-off, Bibb County coroner Lester Chapman ordered an autopsy on Marcia. When tissue samples showed traces of arsenic, the bodies of Ben Lyles, Julia Lyles and Buddy Gabbert were disinterred and samples were taken. All contained copious amounts of arsenic. Brought in for questioning, Anjette had ready explanations for at least three of the deaths. She claimed that she had found Marcia playing with ant poison shortly before she became ill. She also produced a note, which she claimed was from Julia Lyles. In it, Julia confessed to killing her son and said that her own death had been suicide.

The note was an obvious forgery and cut no ice with the Bibb County sheriff, particularly after it emerged that Anjette had personally gained in excess of $50,000 from the deaths. On May 6, Anjette Lyles was arraigned for the murders of Ben Lyles, Buddy Gabber, Julia Lyles and Marcia.

Anjette's would eventually stand trial for only one murder, that of her daughter. However, the prosecution was allowed to present evidence of the other three murders in order to illustrate a pattern. Although mostly circumstantial, that evidence made a compelling argument for Anjette's guilt.

Witnesses testified that Anjette often screamed and swore at her daughter and had on more than one occasion threatened to kill her. Other witnesses had seen Anjette furtively pouring the contents of a bottle into drinks she intended taking to her mother-in-law and daughter at the hospital. A restaurant employee claimed to have examined the contents of the bottle and found it to be ant poison.

Hospital employees said that Anjette's behavior towards her daughter was very odd. While Marcia was suffering hallucinations and screaming about bugs on her skin, Anjette made no effort to comfort the child. Instead, she stood in the corner laughing. On the day (two weeks before her death) that doctors informed Anjette that they expected Marcia to make a full recovery, Anjette went out and ordered a coffin for the girl. The following day she packed up her daughter's belongings and threw away all the flowers that had been brought for her. However, she kept the vases, saying she was going to use them at the funeral.

Other witnesses spoke of flippant remarks made by Anjette as her victims lay dying. In each case, she confidently predicted that the victim would soon be dead.

There was only one witness for the defense, Anjette Lyles herself. She read out a lengthy statement in which she vehemently denied killing her daughter or anyone else. However, her icy demeanor during the trial did nothing to help her case. While complete strangers openly wept in the courtroom as details of Marcia's horrific and painful death were revealed, Anjette remained stone-faced and unmoved. It took the jury just an hour and a half to find her guilty. The judge then pronounced sentence of death.

But Anjette Lyles did not die in the electric chair. The state of Georgia had little appetite for executing a white woman, no matter how horrific her crimes. At the same time, they were acutely aware that a commutation of sentence would likely cause a public backlash. The Georgia Supreme Court, therefore, upheld the death sentence but ordered that Anjette be examined by a panel of medical professionals, including four psychiatrists. These experts declared her to be a paranoid schizophrenic who experienced hallucinations and claimed that she saw angels flying around the room.

Anjette's death sentence was therefore commuted and she was transferred to the state mental hospital in Milledgeville, spending nearly twenty years there until her death of a heart attack on December 4, 1977, at the age of 52.

In a bizarre end to this most unusual case, Anjette Lyles was buried beside two of her victims, her husband Ben and daughter Marcia.

Killing For Comfort

Alice Williams and Norma Davis were friends. The two elderly ladies lived in a quiet, gated community in Canyon Lake, California, and usually checked in with each other regularly. So when Alice hadn't heard from Norma for a few days, she became concerned. The community they lived in was safe, but at 87 years old, Norma might easily have fallen and hurt herself. When Norma failed to answer her phone, Alice decided to check on her.

At around 9 o'clock on the morning of February 14, 1994, Alice knocked on Norma's door. Getting no reply, she waited a few moments and then knocked again. The house remained deathly silent. Her concern growing, Alice turned the door handle and found the door unlocked. This too worried her. Norma was security conscious. Certain now that her friend had met with an accident, Alice entered. She called out her friend's name then began climbing the stairs. Norma was seated in a chair in the upper den, a blanket drawn over her feet. At first, Alice thought she was sleeping but as her eyes adjusted to the light she could make out the wooden handles of two knives. One protruded from

Norma's neck, the other from her chest. Alice staggered down the stairs and called 911.

It did not take long for police and emergency personnel to arrive. As detectives began processing the scene they immediately formed a number of impressions. The attack was vicious, the victim stabbed 11 times, her throat slashed so deeply that her head was nearly severed. This pointed to a personal motive, perhaps a vendetta. Coupled with the fact that there had been no forced entry into the home and that the victim had neither been robbed nor raped, detectives believed that the killer was most likely an acquaintance or family member. One interesting clue left at the scene was the bloody imprint of a sneaker. The print was small, leading the police to conclude that it had been made by a woman. Yet they did not believe that it belonged to the killer. A murder this brutal could not have been committed by a woman, surely?

Following up on the theory that Norma Davis had known her killer, the police queried her friends and family at length. They turned up nothing. The active 87-year-old had been universally liked. No one could understand why anybody would have wanted to harm her.

Two weeks after the murder of Norma Davis, friends and family of June Roberts phoned to congratulate her on her 66th birthday. When their calls went unanswered, three friends drove to her mobile home on Big Tee Drive in Sun City. They found her golf cart standing on the lawn, a bunch of keys that included her house key hanging from the ignition. Letting themselves in, the friends found June lying on the floor in the den, an overturned chair partially covering her body. It appeared from her terrible injuries that she'd been battered to death, a heavy wine decanter the likely murder weapon.

As in the case of Norma Davis, there was no sign of forced entry into the home, leading the police to believe that Norma had known her killer. Again there was no evidence of rape or robbery and police were at a loss as to the motive. They would not, however, comment on speculation that a serial killer was active in the area, preying on elderly residents. The M.O. of the two crimes was significantly different, they insisted.

This assertion would soon prove to be incorrect. Norma Davis had been strangled as well as stabbed and the autopsy on June Roberts would determine that she had not died from the blows to her head as first believed. She'd been strangled to death with a length of telephone cord.

The police had still not admitted a link between the murders when they caught a break in the case, although they didn't realize it at the time. On March 10, 1994, an attractive blonde woman of about 40 walked into The Main Street Trading Post, an antiques store in Lake Elsinore, California. She told the clerk, 57-year-old Dorinda Hawkins, that she was looking for picture frames. Dorinda let her browse, even allowing her into the small workshop at the back of the store. She could not have imagined what would happen next.

As Dorinda stood with her back to the customer, she felt something suddenly pulled tight around her neck. Twisting around she saw that the customer had a length of yellow nylon rope twisted around her throat and was throttling her. Dorinda tried to fight back but the woman, despite standing only 5-foot-2 was remarkably strong. She tried begging and the woman responded by speaking to her in a calm, soothing voice, telling her to relax and calm down. The last thing Dorinda remembered was the woman's cold blue eyes watching her as her struggles weakened and she blacked out.

The sound of a jangling telephone roused Dorinda from unconsciousness. Her throat throbbed and felt raw and swollen. She noticed by the clock on the wall that she'd been out for forty minutes. Staggering to her feet, Dorinda walked towards the phone, which had by now stopped ringing. She picked up the receiver and dialed 911. Dorinda Hawkins had just survived an encounter with a serial killer.

At first, the police did not link the attack to the two murders. Dorinda was younger than the other victims and the motive, in this case, had obviously been robbery. $25 had been taken from the register and Dorinda's purse was also missing from her bag. After being treated, Dorinda worked with a police artist to draw up a composite sketch. The police would soon have a suspect to compare that sketch against.

On March 15, an employee at June Roberts' bank phoned Mrs. Roberts' daughter to report suspicious activity on her credit card. The card had been used after Mrs. Roberts' death. As police questioned staff at the stores where the card was used, a familiar theme began to emerge. All of them described a petite blond woman with shoulder length hair, a dead ringer for the woman who had attacked Dorinda Hawkins. Further inquiries gave the police a name, a former registered nurse named Dana Sue Gray.

Gray was placed under surveillance and the police noted with interest that, since the composite sketch had appeared in the local papers, she'd cut her hair short and died it red. They also learned that Gray had known both Norma Davis and June Roberts. Armed with this evidence, the police pulled Gray in for questioning on June 16. That same day, another elderly woman was found bludgeoned to death in her home.

Dora Beebe, 87, had failed to turn up for a lunch date with a male acquaintance. Acutely aware of the recent murders in the area, he'd gone to her house to check on her. He'd found the door unlocked and Mrs. Beebe dead on the bathroom floor. Even by the standards of the previous murders, this one was incredibly brutal. The elderly woman had been battered to death with an iron, the attack so vicious that when the body was removed to the morgue, the victim's shape could still be seen on the floor, outlined in blood.

The police, meanwhile, had executed a search warrant on the home that Gray shared with her boyfriend and his 5-year-old son. They unearthed a wealth of evidence, including clothes, jewelry, and perfume bought with the victims' credit cards. They also found June Roberts' bank book, showing a $2,000 withdrawal made on the day Mrs. Roberts was killed. It would later emerge that Gray had gone on a shopping spree immediately after the murder, treating herself to a perm, beauty treatments, and an expensive lunch. She'd also bought clothes, perfume, liquor and gourmet foods, as well as toys for her boyfriend's son. The child had, in fact, accompanied Gray to Mrs. Roberts' home, waiting in the car while Gray was inside, stabbing and throttling the old lady.

Under interrogation, Gray offered a ludicrous explanation for how she'd come into possession of June Roberts' credit card. She said that she'd visited Mrs. Roberts at her home and found her murdered. Rather than calling the police, she'd rifled through Mrs. Roberts' purse and taken her credit card to go on a shopping spree. "I get desperate to buy things," she explained. "Shopping puts me at rest. I'm lost without it."

Dana Sue Gray went on trial for murder on March 10, 1995. She initially entered an insanity plea, but faced with the prospect of execution, she admitted to killing June Roberts and Dora Beebe. No charges were brought in the Davis murder due to lack of evidence. Gray is also suspected of three other murders, in Riverside and San Diego.

She is currently incarcerated at the California Women's Prison in Chowchilla, where she will remain for the rest of her natural life.

In Satan's Name

Welkom is a small town of some 200,000 inhabitants in South Africa's Free State province. This is gold mining country, with many of the residents employed by the local mines. They are a conservative bunch by nature, god-fearing and obsessed with the sport of rugby. It is hardly the kind of place where you'd expect a ritualistic murder to occur. Yet, in April 2011, that is exactly what happened, a crime so horrific in its execution that it rocked the close-knit community to its very core.

Michael van Eck was a handsome 24-year-old who worked at the Beatrix Gold Mine. He was a happy and outgoing young man, liked by all who knew him. The only thing missing in his life was a significant other. He just hadn't found the right girl yet. Now, though, he thought he might have addressed that problem. A few weeks earlier, he'd met a pretty, dark-haired, art student on the social networking site 2Go. Her name was Chane van Heerden, and through their online chats, Michael had discovered that they shared many of the same interests. Eventually, he'd plucked up the courage to ask her out.

On Friday, April 16, Michael excitedly told his boss that Chane had agreed to go on a date with him. "That's great news," the boss responded. "Where are you taking her?"

"I was thinking dinner and a movie," Michael said. "Although she wants to meet up at the graveyard."

"The graveyard?" Michael's boss said frowning, to which Michael could only shrug. The boss let it go at that. Who could understand young people these days?

Michael van Eck's boss thought no more of his employee's strange date until Monday morning when Michael failed to show up for work. That was unusual, and after phoning Michael's home and getting no reply, the boss began to worry. When calls to friends and family turned up no clues as to Michael's whereabouts, his boss called the police.

It was obvious where they should begin their search. After Michael's boss shared his story about the graveyard rendezvous, units were dispatched to the cemetery with sniffer dogs, hoping to find some trace of the young man. They found a lot more than that. The dogs had barely hit the ground when they picked up a scent. It led officers almost immediately to a shallow grave, where the headless corpse of Michael van Eck lay buried. There were other mutilations too. The right arm was missing, and both legs had been severed at the knee.

It did not take the police long to trace Michael's date. Chane van Heerden shared an apartment with her boyfriend, 24-year-old Maartens van der Merwe, in the suburb of St. Helena. Entering the residence was like entering another realm. Chane's macabre artworks decorated the walls, some depicted demons, others what appeared to be animal fetuses, still others eerily rendered portraits of Chane. There were books on Satanism and the occult. And then there was Chane's diary in which she described (among other things) her love for stitching human skin. Yet even those were not the most horrific of the discoveries. Not by a long shot. Buried in the garden the police found Michael van Eck's missing arm, and one of his feet. In another hole, they found the mutilated remains of several cats. Michael's head was discovered in another makeshift grave, all of the facial skin flayed. That skin would be found stashed in the refrigerator, the eye sockets and mouth sewed closed with thick yarn.

Under interrogation, the murderous couple made little attempt to cover up their involvement in the horrendous crime. They admitted to being avowed Satanists and said they had been killing and mutilating animals for some time before they decided to take things to the next level and carry out the murder. Chane had started trolling the 2GO site with the express intention of finding a victim. She'd started corresponding with Michael, eventually luring him to a meeting at the cemetery. There, Maartens van der Merwe had lain in wait.

Michael was overpowered and killed. His corpse was then mutilated, with the head, arm and foot carried from the scene and the rest of the body interred in a shallow grave. Back at her apartment, Chane had first sewn the eyes and mouth shut and then flayed the skin from the face in a bizarre death mask. No explanation was given for the mutilation, although Chane wrote in her diary, "I will tear their faces off to see the truth."

The defendants were tried separately for their roles in the murder. At van der Merwe's trial, it was revealed that he was a diagnosed schizophrenic, who had stopped taking his medication at the time of the murder. The judge appeared to have some empathy with him, depicting him as the passive partner in the relationship, controlled and manipulated by his girlfriend. Nonetheless, the sentence was the harshest allowable by law – life in prison.

Chane van Heerden stood trial on November 2011, pleading guilty to all charges and spending the entire time wearing a smirk on her face. The judge was less sympathetic in her case. "I have no doubts about the danger you pose to society," he said in his summing up. "You are a dangerous criminal and you may not apply for parole until you have served 20 years behind bars." Chane van Heerden was sentenced to 20 years to life.

The Crippen Case

The case of Dr. Hawley Harvey Crippen is one of the most famous in the annals of British crime and goes down in history as the first case where radio was used to apprehend the suspect.

Crippen was, in fact, an American, born in Coldwater, Michigan, on September 11, 1862. As a young man, he qualified as a homeopathic doctor, obtaining a diploma from the Medical College of Philadelphia. A couple of years later, in 1885, he qualified as an eye and ear specialist, certified by the Ophthalmic Hospital in New York. That same year Crippen traveled to England but found that his qualifications were insufficient to gain accreditation there. He then returned to the United States where he spent the next five years traveling and practicing as a doctor in several cities. At some time during that period, he married and fathered a son. However, his wife Charlotte died of apoplexy in 1892. Crippen, unable to care for his son, sent the child to be raised by his maternal grandparents in California.

A short while after relieving himself of his parental responsibilities, Crippen traveled to New York, where he met a buxom 17-year-old named Cora Turner. Cora's real name was Kunigunde Mackamotski, and she was the daughter of a Russian Pole father and a German mother. Despite her tender years, she was worldly, precocious and demanding. She was being kept by a wealthy businessman at the time she met Crippen, but she took a shine to the young doctor and soon abandoned her sugar daddy. She and Crippen married on September 1, 1892.

The new Mrs. Crippen was the polar opposite of Crippen's first wife. Whereas Charlotte had been demure and almost puritanical, Cora was loud, bossy and sexually demanding. She also fancied herself as an opera singer and despite a meager talent insisted that Crippen pay for her singing lessons, something her former lover had done. The couple traveled for a while, taking in St. Louis, Philadelphia, and Toronto. Then Crippen landed a job with the Munyon Company, a patent medicine business. In 1900 Munyon sent him to England, to manage their London office.

The Crippens quickly settled into life in the UK, with Crippen working from Munyon's offices on London's Shaftesbury Avenue, and Cora pursuing a music hall career, performing under the stage name Belle Elmore. She was mainly unsuccessful in this pursuit, blaming Crippen's lack of support for her failure. She did, however, make many friends within the music hall community and had several sexual liaisons including with American performer, Bruce Miller. Crippen probably knew of his wife's indiscretions but turned a blind eye. A timid man, standing just 5-foot-4, he was intimidated by his wife, both physically and emotionally.

In 1902, Crippen lost his job at Munyon and with it his £10,000 per annum salary. Over the years that followed, he worked at a number of jobs including as a dentist and a "women's consultant." Eventually, he returned to Munyon but their business was by now in decline and Crippen departed again. This time, he found work with Yale Tooth Specialists and it was while working there that he employed a pretty, young typist named Ethel le Neve.

Ethel, who had been raised by a brutish, alcoholic father was desperate for any kind of affection and she was soon attracted to the gentle, kind-hearted Dr. Crippen. By 1905, the two had become lovers and Crippen was promising to leave his wife. However, he made no move to do so. As he often explained to Ethel, he was afraid that Cora might respond violently.

In January 1910, the Crippens moved to a large house at 39 Hilldrop Crescent, Camden Town. Why Crippen chose such a large property is unknown. He was by now working for himself, hawking patent medicines and the £58 10s annual rental on the house must have stretched his declared earnings. Yet, the Crippens were hardly destitute. Cora still paraded around in jewels and furs and the couple had some £600 in a joint bank account, a considerable sum in those days.

Cora Crippen, despite her meager success on stage, was by now a well-known figure in theatrical circles. For two years before her death, she was Honorary Treasurer of the Music Hall Ladies Guild. Those who knew her described her as vivacious and pleasant, loud and outgoing. They wondered what had ever attracted her to the introverted Crippen, a small, balding man with prominent eyes behind gold-rimmed spectacles. They seemed the quintessential odd couple.

By December 1909, Cora must have been thinking the same thing. She knew that her husband had a mistress and while that didn't bother her too much, she had tired of the marriage and wanted out. Not that Crippen would have expended much energy trying to stop her, but Cora was not prepared to walk away empty handed. She wanted the £600 in their joint savings account and on December 15, 1909, she gave notice of withdrawal to their bank.

One can only imagine how this must have affected Crippen. He was the one who had earned that money, traversing some tough times to do so. He'd supported his wife during her quest for stardom, funding singing lessons and theater productions. He'd bankrolled her lavish spending on furs and jewels. Now she was intent on walking away with everything he had in the world. Crippen had never had the guts to stand up to his wife before. He was determined to do so now.

On January 17, 1910, Crippen ordered five grains of hyocine hydrobromide from Lewis and Burrow in New Oxford Street. The chemists did not have a sufficient quantity of the deadly drug in stock and had to order it from the wholesalers. Crippen collected his order on January 19.

On January 31, 1910, the Crippens hosted a dinner party at their Hilldrop Crescent home, for retired music-hall performer Paul Martinetti and his wife. After dinner, the Martinettis and Crippens played several games of whist before the Martinettis left at around 1:30 a.m. It was the last time anyone but Crippen saw Cora alive.

The next day, Crippen pawned one of Cora's diamond rings and a pair of earrings for £80. On February 3, two letters signed "Belle Elmore" arrived at the Music Hall Ladies Guild. In them, Cora Crippen resigned her position as Honorary Treasurer, explaining that she had been summoned to the US to attend a sick relative. The letters were not in Cora's hand. When questioned about this by Mrs. Martinetti, Crippen said that Cora had asked him to write the letters as she had left in a hurry and had not had time herself.

Crippen pawned more of Cora's jewelry on February 20. That same evening, he caused a minor scandal by taking Ethel le Neve to the ball of the Music Hall Ladies Benevolent Fund. Cora's friends were angered to see Ethel wearing a broach they recognized as belonging to Cora. If Crippen noticed their reaction, he seemed unaffected by it. By March 1910, Ethel le Neve had moved into 39 Hilldrop Crescent.

At the end of March, Crippen gave his landlord three months notice of his intention to vacate the property. Just before Easter 1910, he told Mrs. Martinetti that Cora was seriously ill in the US and was not expected to live. On March 24, he sent Mrs. Martinetti a telegram. "Belle died yesterday at 6pm," it read. Crippen had meanwhile taken Ethel to France for a holiday.

Crippen's behavior since his wife's unexpected departure had been less than discreet, causing a great deal of discussion among Cora's friends. Several of them were angered at seeing Ethel le Neve parading around in Cora's furs and jewelry while others already suspected that Dr. Crippen was not being entirely honest about Cora's disappearance. When an actor friend of Cora's traveled to the United States he made inquiries about Cora and turned up nothing. Returning to London, he visited Scotland Yard and reported that he believed Crippen had murdered his wife.

A week after that report, Chief Inspector Walter Dew visited Crippen at his place of work. Crippen admitted that he had not been truthful about his wife's disappearance. Cora was very much alive, he said. She'd eloped to Chicago to be with an old friend from her music hall days, Bruce Miller. The entire story about her death had been concocted to spare Crippen the shame and embarrassment of his wife's elopement. Dew then asked Crippen if he could search the Hilldrop Crescent property and Crippen readily agreed. Dew found nothing to suggest that Crippen was telling anything but the truth. He almost felt pity for the timid little man. If Crippen had held his nerve, he'd likely have gotten away with murder.

But the attentions of the police had shaken Crippen up and he made the fateful decision to flee. That same night, he and Ethel boarded a steamer for Antwerp, with Ethel disguised as a boy and posing as Crippen's son.

On July 11, Inspector Dew returned to the Crippen house to verify a detail regarding Cora's departure. He wanted to know when Cora had left for America. Finding no one home, Dew questioned the neighbors who informed him that Crippen had left days before, destination unknown.

His suspicions now roused, Dew acted immediately. Crippen and le Neve's description was widely circulated, while Dew returned to Hilldrop Crescent to carry out a more thorough search of the property. That search lasted for several days, during which investigators rummaged through closets, tore back sections of wallpaper and dug up the garden. Eventually, their search led them down to the cellar and it was there that they made a gory discovery, chunks of flesh, shallowly buried, wrapped in a man's pajama top and covered in quicklime. Cora's remains amounted to pieces of skin, a buttock, the abdominal organs and chunks of muscle flesh. She was identified by a scar on a piece of flesh from the abdomen.

While this was going on, Crippen and le Neve were steaming their way across the Atlantic aboard the SS Montrose, bound for Canada. Crippen was posing as John Philo Robinson, a merchant, le Neve as his 16-year-old son. Crippen said that they were traveling to California where they planned to settle for the sake of his son's health. The story, however, was believed by few on board, least of all Captain Kendall, who couldn't help noticing the "boy's" feminine features and curvy figure.

These suspicions were further roused when Kendall was leafing through a copy of the London Daily Mail and found a story about the Crippen murder, along with pictures of the fugitives. The Montrose was at that point 150 miles from England, the furthest distance over which a wireless message could be transmitted. Realizing that time was of the essence, Kendall immediately sent a message to his company's offices in London. They, in turn, forwarded the details to Inspector Dew at Scotland Yard.

The following day, Dew boarded the SS Laurentic, bound for Canada out of Liverpool. The Laurentic was a faster ship than the Montrose and was expected to pass the latter in mid-ocean. Dew would, therefore, beat Crippen to Canada and be waiting there to arrest him. The operation was carried out in secrecy but word of it leaked to the newspapers. Over the days the followed, tabloids on both sides of the Atlantic carried stories of the unfolding drama to an eager readership. Crippen and le Neve meanwhile were totally oblivious to their impending arrest and whiled away their time on deck, behaving more like a courting couple than the father and son they were supposed to be.

On July 27, the Laurentic overtook the slower moving Montrose, the two ships passing within sight of one another. Then, on July 31, Dew, along with members of the Quebec police boarded the Montrose as she lay moored off Father Point.

Crippen was standing on deck when Dew approached him. "Good morning, Dr. Crippen," Dew said. "I am Inspector Dew of Scotland Yard. I believe you know me." Crippen barely hesitated before replying in a low voice. "Good Morning, Mr. Dew."

Crippen and le Neve were returned to London under guard, he charged with murder, she with being an accessory after the fact.

The Crippen case opened before Chief Justice Lord Alverstone at the Old Bailey on October 18, 1910. Testimony presented at the trial revealed the meticulous manner in which Crippen had disposed of his wife's body. After killing her, he removed her bones and limbs, which he burned in the kitchen stove. Her organs were dissolved in acid in the bathtub, while her head was placed in a handbag and thrown overboard during a day trip to Dieppe, France. Why exactly Crippen chose to bury the rest of the remains was never explained.

The trial lasted five days but, from the start, there was little doubt as to the outcome. Crippen, in any case, seemed to have accepted his fate. His sole intent appeared to be to protect Ethel le Neve. In the end, it took the jury just 27 minutes to find him guilty. He was sentenced to death by hanging. Four days later, Ethel le Neve was found not guilty as an accessory.

Hawley Harvey Crippen went to the gallows at Pentonville Prison on November 23, 1910. His last request was that a photograph of Ethel le Neve be buried with him and this was granted.

Ethel le Neve sailed for New York on the morning of Crippen's execution. She returned to London after the First World War and later married a man named Stanley Smith. She died in 1967, at the age of 84.

The Waterfront Ripper

The night clerk looked up with distaste at the couple standing before him. The man was short and stocky with sandy hair. He was wearing a cheap coat and a dirty peaked cap. The clerk guessed his age to be about mid-thirties, like his companion, a chubby dark-haired woman. She wore a black coat with a ring of fake fur around the neck. She reeked of cheap perfume. They both reeked of whiskey. Still, it wasn't his place to judge, the hotel, just off the Embarcedero on San Francisco's waterfront, was hardly the Ritz. The couple before him was typical of the establishment's clientele. The man asked for a room, paid cash and signed the register in the name of Mr. and Mrs. H. Myers of San Francisco. Later, the clerk would describe two distinctive characteristics to the police. The man had "sleepy blue eyes," he said, and a small, pointy nose.

The couple checked in at around three o'clock on the morning of Saturday, April 6, 1935. At around 5:30, the man reappeared and asked the clerk where he could buy sandwiches and some liquor. The clerk told him that he wouldn't be able to buy liquor at this hour, but that sandwiches might be purchased at an all-night diner nearby. The man then left the hotel, saying he'd be back soon. He never returned.

By checkout time the following morning, the pudgy woman had still not put in an appearance. A maid was sent to rouse her and returned ashen face and barely able to speak. When the receptionist went up to the room to investigate, he found the woman lying on the blood-drenched bed. She'd been viciously stabbed and beaten, her mouth sealed with adhesive tape to stop her screaming. The coroner would later determine that she'd been dead approximately eight hours, which coincided with the departure of her companion. The body had been slashed and stabbed with a razor while she was still alive. Death, though, was due to strangulation. The killer had taken the time to wipe the crime scene of any prints, dashing police hopes for an early arrest.

The police did, however, have a solid description of the suspect, courtesy of the night clerk. He described the man as blond, five-foot-three, 160 pounds. He had a sharp nose and blue eyes, set in a pudgy face. "Like a fat fox," was the descriptor use by the clerk, who also noted that the suspect walked with the distinctive rolling gait of a seafarer.

As officers fanned out to search the waterfront for their man, an identification came in on the victim. Her name was Betty Coffin and she was well known to the police as a prostitute, dope dealer, and con artist, usually working with her husband, Ernie. The pair was known on the street as "Cat and Mouse."

The police immediately launched a search for Ernie "The Mouse" Coffin, tracking him eventually to a Gough Street flophouse. Ernie had no idea who had killed his wife. His best bet was that it might have been rival drug dealers.

The police, meanwhile, were having no luck tracking down their suspect, but they began to believe that he might be the same man who was responsible for a series of five rape-murders committed in San Diego between 1931 and 1934. Those crimes, bearing a similar M.O., remained unsolved.

Months passed and the trail eventually went cold. The murder of Betty Coffin was consigned to the unsolved pile, while the police worked fresher cases.

On Tuesday, June 25, 1940, San Francisco detectives Ahern and Engler were summoned to the scene of a brutal murder at a downtown hotel. The victim was a petite, blond woman with a boyish haircut. She'd been strangled and slashed with a razor, which had been left behind by the killer. As in the Coffin case, the scene had been wiped clean of fingerprints.

Questioning the clerk, police learned that the victim (identified as Irene Chandler, a known prostitute) had checked into the hotel at 4 o'clock the previous afternoon. She'd been accompanied by a man, and his description sounded familiar – short and stocky with a small pointy nose and "sleepy blue eyes." The Waterfront Ripper was back.

The detectives' next move followed a logical piece of deduction. As the couple had arrived at the hotel during the afternoon, detectives believed that they'd likely met at a nearby bar. Following up on this theory, 100 police officers were dispatched to local taverns to question staff and customers. Eight days later, they had their first break.

At a bar a couple of blocks from the murder scene, Detective Ahern found a woman who claimed to know the murder victim. Furthermore, she said that she knew the man who had been drinking with the victim on the day of the murder. His name was Harry and he was a friend of her husband. However, that was where the woman's recollection ended. She didn't know Harry's last name, where he lived, or what ships he might have worked on. She also didn't know where her husband was, claiming she hadn't seen him for months. After much pressing, Ahern finally managed to glean a tiny scrap of information from her. She thought that Harry might have worked with her husband aboard a ship called the Monterey.

Armed with this tenuous lead, Ahern visited the offices of the Matson Line and asked them for a list of all sailors named Harry who had worked aboard the Monterey in the last five years. He took that list - numbering 20 – to the Sailor's Union offices, and compared it against their records, narrowing the list to eight and then eventually to one - Harry W. Gordon. A 35-year-old merchant seaman, Gordon's description closely matched that of the murder suspect. Further inquiries tracked him to Los Angeles, where he was arrested on July 8, 1940, while attending a Sailor's Union meeting.

Gordon was booked on suspicion of murder but steadfastly denied any involvement in the Coffin and Chandler killings. He stuck to his guns until Detectives Ahern and Engler arrived from San Francisco to question him. Then, after just a few minutes of cursory interrogation, he suddenly blurted. "Okay, I'm the man you want. I killed those girls. And I might as well tell you because you'll find out anyway. I killed my wife in New York back in '33."

The police were stunned by this admission, but further investigation revealed that Gordon's estranged wife, Florence, had indeed been murdered and that her killing closely resembled the other two cases. She'd been strangled into submission and then slashed with a razor. She had bled to death on the floor of her apartment.

Gordon claimed that he'd killed his wife after an argument about child support payments. The memory of the murder, he said, had stayed with him and when he'd found himself alone in the hotel room with Betty Coffin he'd been struck by a "blue flash, like electricity." He couldn't remember killing either of the women, only coming out of his trance to find them lying dead and bleeding on the floor. "I felt terrible afterwards," he wailed.

Gordon swore that the three murders that he'd confessed to, were the only one's he'd committed and that he knew nothing of the San Diego murders. "I have nothing to hide," he said. "And I don't want to hurt any more women, so let them gas me and be done with it."

By the time he went on trial, though, Gordon had changed his tune, pleading not guilty by reason of insanity. It did him no good. Found guilty, he was sentenced to death.

Harry Gordon was executed in the gas chamber at San Quentin on September 5, 1941.

Hell's Sanitarium

Compared to most industrialized nations, Canada has a relatively low crime rate and an even lower rate of violent crime. Still, America's northern neighbor has produced some truly horrendous killers. Like Paul Bernardo, the depraved torture slayer of young girls, including his own sister-in-law; or horrific child killer Clifford Olson; or Robert Pickton, the British Columbia farmer who murdered a reported 49 prostitutes and fed them to his pigs. None of these killers, sickening though their crimes were, can quite compare to Lila and William Young, a couple most Canadians have likely never heard of.

Lila Coolen Young was a graduate of the National School of Obstetrics and Midwifery. Her husband, William, claimed to be a doctor and an ordained minister of the Seventh Day Adventist church. The pair were outwardly deeply religious and moral, devoted to helping others. To facilitate this, they founded the Life and Health Sanitarium in a small cottage in East Chester, Nova Scotia, in 1928, when Lila was 29 and William 30. The facility was not a success and they barely managed to scrape a living from the handful of patients they were able to attract. The Youngs wanted more and soon struck on an idea to fill their coffers.

The practice of baby farming had been the bane of unwed mothers and their illegitimate offspring across the British Empire during the 19th century. It involved women who were prepared to take in unwanted babies for a weekly stipend or a lump sum payment. Many baby farmers were honest in their endeavors, but there were others, women like Amelia Dyer and Annie Walters, who murdered their young charges and pocketed the money paid for their upkeep. At the time that the Youngs struck on their money making scheme in the 1920's, baby farming had been outlawed in England and other parts of the Empire for decades. But Canada, with its strict abortion and birth control laws, was still ripe for the picking. The Youngs saw their opportunity and seized it.

The Life and Health Sanitarium was rechristened the Ideal Maternity Home and Sanitarium. Shortly after, the Youngs began discreetly putting out the word about the services they were offering. An unwed mother-to-be could book into the sanitarium for a short stay, during which she'd give birth and later leave without her baby. The child would then be put up for adoption while the young mother would return to her hometown with her reputation intact.

It was an arrangement that suited everyone concerned, but the Youngs did not offer their services out of the goodness of their hearts. Their charges were steep. A married woman could give birth at the facility and spend two weeks recuperating for a payment of $75. But unwed mothers were desperate and, therefore, easy to fleece. For them, the fee ranged from $100 to

$200 plus extra costs for supplies and medicines. Then there were additional charges for arranging the adoption. All in all, the total bill could easily run to $300, an outrageous sum for the 1920's. Many mothers couldn't afford the full amount. To them, the Youngs offered a ready solution. They could pay off the balance by working at the sanitarium. This provided the Youngs with a steady supply of unpaid domestic labor.

The maternity business was lucrative for the Youngs, but it was just a sideline compared to their primary source of income. The real money was to be made in selling babies.

By placing adverts in American newspapers and magazines, the Youngs attracted untold childless couples from New York and New Jersey to their Nova Scotia facility. Many of these were wealthy Jewish couples, who were prohibited by the laws of the era from adopting non-Jewish babies. Lila and William Young had no problem breaking that rule. If they said a baby was Jewish, then it was. The prospective parents, desperate to adopt, asked few questions. The Canadian authorities asked none at all.

The baby-selling business was extremely profitable. During the 1920's the Youngs charged $1,000 for a baby. By the time their business was at its peak in the 1940's the price had risen to $10,000. In the interim, their modest sanitarium had grown from a tiny cottage to a sprawling 54-room facility. In the intervening years, they'd banked in excess of $3 million.

So far there seems to be little wrong with what the Youngs were doing. In fact, it could be argued that they were providing a

valuable service, sparing unwed mothers from shame and
humiliation, providing homes for unwanted babies, bringing the
joy of parenthood to childless couples. But the Youngs had little
interest in altruistic considerations. Their operation was a
business, and the children that passed through their hands were
mere stock. The couple had strict quality requirements for this
"stock" and if a baby did not measure up, for example, if it had a
deformity, if it were sickly, if it were bi-racial, they simply
disposed of it. How many such children died at their hands?
Conservative estimates put the number at 400 to 600, which
would easily place the Youngs among the most heinous killers in
history.

And the children's deaths were not easy. Unwilling to get their
hands dirty, the Youngs sectioned these "unwanteds" off from the
rest of their stock and then systematically starved them to death.
The babies were fed nothing but water and molasses. Most died
within two weeks.

Such wholesale slaughter, however, could not remain under wraps
forever. Rumors about dead babies and about the conditions at the
home began to circulate. In 1933, the Office of Public Health asked
Dr. Frank Roy Davis to look into it. That ongoing investigation
eventually led to William and Lila Young being charged with two
counts of manslaughter in March 1936. These charges related to
the deaths of Eva Nieforth and her newborn baby, due to
negligence and unsanitary conditions.

But the Youngs were both cleared of wrongdoing and acquitted.
Many believed that they had dirt on local politicians who had

made use of their services. That would certainly explain why the authorities turned a blind eye to their activities for so long.

Dr. Davis, though, was not so easily dissuaded. He asked the Royal Canadian Mounted Police (RCMP) to look into every recorded death at the home during the time the Youngs were operating it. The findings were quite astonishing. It emerged that the Ideal Maternity Home had an infant mortality rate of 8.1%, more than double the Nova Scotia average of 3%. But even that was just the tip of the iceberg. It referred only to reported cases. The vast majority of the deaths that occurred at the sanitarium were never reported. They were handled "in-house."

The method of disposal would emerge years later after the maternity home was shut down, when a former handyman at the facility finally decided to speak up. Glen Shatford said that some of the tiny corpses were tossed into the sea or incinerated in a furnace. Most, however, were buried, with cardboard butter boxes obtained from a local grocer serving as makeshift coffins. When the case eventually broke in the media the tiny victims would be dubbed the "Butterbox Babies."

Shatford went further, revealing that it was Lila Young alone who decided which baby would live and which would die. She'd walk through the maternity ward inspecting her "stock" with a practiced eye. Any infant that did not meet her definition of quality was sectioned off to be systematically starved to death. It is difficult to conceive how an individual, let alone a woman and trained midwife, could have acted so callously.

Eventually, in 1945, the authorities decided to act, although it was not the police who came calling, but public health officials arriving to carry out an inspection. What they found shocked them. The wards were filthy, with grime-encrusted floors and walls, the bedding had not been changed in weeks, swarms of large black flies settled on every surface.

But that was far from the worst of it. In another room, inspectors found dozens of severely undernourished babies, living in the most horrendous conditions. Some wailed helplessly against their thirst and hunger, others had already given up and lay with sunken eyes and bloated bellies, waiting on an inevitable death. The stench of urine and feces pervaded the place and flies settled on everything, especially on the helpless infants. These were the children that had failed Lila Young's "quality assessment." Outraged, the inspectors issued a citation on the spot and arranged for the babies to be moved to another facility.

William and Lila Young would eventually be tried and found guilty of multiple health code violations. The penalty? A ludicrous $150 fine. However, there was a more serious consequence for them. Partially as a result of their case, the government beefed up the licensing regulations for maternity homes. The Youngs were forced to re-apply for a license and when they did, their application was refused. Not that it bothered them much. They continued operating their home without a license, brazenly advertising "Lovely Babies for Adoption."

The Youngs again fell foul of the law in 1946, when they were convicted of selling babies to four American couples. Again the sanction was ridiculously lenient, a fine that amounted to just

$428. As they'd sold the babies for $10,000 each, their profit after paying the fine was $39,572.

But their heinous activities were about to catch up with the Youngs and in the best possible illustration of poetic justice it would come about at their own hands. Lila Young was angered by the media coverage of their trial and decided to file a libel suit against a local newspaper. The paper fought back, using its reach to highlight the filthy conditions at their facility, the malnourished babies, the children who had simply vanished. By the time the Youngs libel suit was dismissed, their reputation, and that of their facility lay in tatters. Their baby farming empire had finally been exposed for the heartless, mercenary operation that it was.

Unfortunately, at that stage, there was no evidence of the wholesale slaughter that had occurred at the home. The Youngs were allowed to close down their facility and shuffle off to a comfortable retirement in Quebec. William Young died of cancer in 1962, Lila Young of leukemia in 1967. It was only after their deaths that Glen Shatford's revelations would lead police to various Nova Scotia fields. By then, the corpses they found were so degraded that it was impossible to prove cause of death.

Nightrider & Lady Sundown

On the evening of September 29, 1982, the DeKalb County Sheriff's Office in Fort Payne, Alabama, answered a call giving details to the location of "a young girl's body." The dispatcher was at first skeptical. A similar call had recently been made to the police in nearby Rome, Georgia, and a search had turned up nothing. Nonetheless, it wasn't her job to analyze the reliability of tip-offs. She passed the information on to detectives.

Deputy James Mays took a team to the location that same night, and this time, the tip proved accurate. Lisa Millican, a 13-year-old who had gone missing from the Riverbend Mall in Rome four days earlier, was found at the bottom of a ravine, slumped over a fallen tree. She had been shot, but evidence suggested that she'd been subjected to prolonged torture prior to her death. An autopsy would later reveal that she'd also been raped.

Two items, discovered at the scene, interested investigators. The first was a bloodstained pair of woman's jeans that did not belong

to Lisa. The second was a cluster of three syringes. Because locals
used the area around the crime scene as an informal garbage
dump, it was impossible to tell what, if any, significance these
items held. Investigators sent them to the Alabama Department of
Forensic Science in Huntsville for analysis. The syringes would
prove to have contained a domestic drain cleaner. The blood on
the jeans would be matched to Lisa Millican. None of these clues
gave any idea as to the identity of the killer.

Because Lisa Millican had gone missing from Rome, it was decided
from the outset that detectives there should lead the investigation.
They had, in fact, already opened up a missing persons docket and
turned up some interesting information. Lisa was a resident of the
Harpst Home, a facility for troubled girls. She had a history of
absconding from the home and it was initially believed that she'd
run away. Tragically, this belief was now proven to be false.

The murder investigation fell to Detective Kenneth Kines and he
soon brought himself up to date with the sad, short life of Lisa
Millican. Removed from her parents' home because of accusations
of sexual abuse, she'd been in and out of care facilities and foster
homes. She was known to be sexually precocious, and at times
aggressive towards other girls. No one, however, had any idea who
might have wanted her dead.

Kines next turned his attention to the anonymous phone call that
had revealed the location of Lisa's body. The caller had been
female, and she'd used a peculiar expression, referring to Lisa, as
"on run" a slang term used by inmates of the juvenile justice
system to describe a runaway. The caller, Kines concluded,
probably had a juvenile record.

It wasn't much to go on and Kines was already anticipating weeks and months of wading through juvenile records when he caught an amazingly fortuitous break. A man named John Hancock was being led into the police station to make a statement regarding the abduction of his girlfriend, Janice Kay Chatman. Kines just happened to be listening to the tape as Hancock passed his office. "That's her!" Hancock exclaimed on hearing the voice, "That's the woman who shot me!"

The story that Hancock had to tell seemed barely believable. He said that a young woman driving a brown car with cream stripes had approached him and Janice. She asked if they wanted to go for a ride and although she was a complete stranger, they agreed. (Hancock later explained to police that the woman said she was lonely and, as a Christian, he felt obliged to help her. He also said that he did not feel threatened because there were two small children in the car.)

As they drove around town the woman got into a conversation with someone on a CB radio. She used the handle Lady Sundown and referred to the person on the other end as Nightrider. After a while, Lady Sundown stopped beside a road on the outskirts of town. A moment later, a Red Chevy Granada pulled up behind them and a huge man got out. He introduced himself as Nightrider, then told Lady Sundown to follow him, as he was going to buy some booze. They set off in convoy, with Nightrider making so many twists and turns that John was soon hopelessly disorientated.

Eventually, they came to a stop, whereupon John got out of the car to urinate. He'd taken only a few steps towards the nearby bushes when Lady Sundown walked up behind him, pushed a gun into his back and told him to keep walking. She forced him down a narrow path, walking him a short distance, all the while telling him not to worry about his girlfriend. Then John heard Nightrider yell at her to get it over with. In the next moment, he heard a bang and felt a sharp pain in his shoulder. He went down and lay still. A moment later, he heard car engines start up. When he was sure that they had gone he stumbled back to the road and managed to flag down a trucker who drove him to the nearest police station.

Bizarre though the story seemed, it was Kines only lead and he quickly got Hancock to provide a description of Nightrider, Lady Sundown, and their vehicles. Then another piece of the puzzle slotted into place. Bill Whitner of the Floyd County Sheriff's Department told Kines about a firebombing and drive-by shooting he was investigating. Kines interest was piqued when he heard that a female caller had phoned the sheriff's department both before and after the attacks. Interestingly, the targets were both employees of Rome's Youth Development Center.

Kines next move was to visit the Rome YDC. The female caller's accent suggested that she was not from Georgia, so Kines asked for a list of all the girls who'd been placed in the YDC from out of state. That gave him a list of 25 names and over the next few days he narrowed it down to just one: Judith Ann Neelley. Placing Neelley's picture into a photo array, Kines then showed it to John Hancock and also to Debbie Smith, a young girl who'd escaped an attempted abduction. Both picked out Neelley without hesitation.

A search was now launched for Neelley and it didn't take long before the police had her in custody. She was arrested at a motel in Murfreesboro, Tennessee, on October 9, after attempting to pass a stolen check. Her husband Alvin was arrested a few days later. He was an exact match for the description of Nightrider.

With the suspects in custody, Kines set off for Murfreesboro, prepared for long hours of interrogation in order to try and extract a confession. It didn't turn out that way. Alvin Neelley immediately waived his right to remain silent and gave a detailed statement in which he portrayed Judith as the mastermind behind the abduction / murders. He also provided police with the location of Janice Chatman's body but insisted that he'd been forced into participating in the rapes and murders by Judith. "She's a very dangerous person," he said.

Judith Neelly, meanwhile, was making a confession of her own. She readily admitted to the shooting and firebombing incidents, claiming she had carried them out in revenge for sexual abuse she'd suffered at the YDC. Then, in chilling detail, she told of the abductions and murders of Lisa Millican and Janice Chatman.

Lisa, she said, had been selected because she reminded her of Joanie Cunningham, a character from the TV show "Happy Days." The girl had left the Riverbend Mall with her willingly. Over the days that followed, they drove around aimlessly during the day with Judith's two young children in the back seat, and spent nights at various motels, where Alvin repeatedly raped the girl. When Lisa asked to return to the Habst home, the Neeleys took to handcuffing her to the bed at night. Eventually, they decided to kill Lisa, to prevent her reporting the abduction and rapes.

Driving to Rocky Glade, in DeKalb County, Judith ordered Lisa out
of the car and walked her to a secluded spot. She told Lisa that she
was going to give her an injection to knock her out so that she
(Judith) could make her escape. Instead, she injected Liquid Drano
into the girl's neck. Judith believed that the injection would kill
Lisa but instead it only caused the teenager to suffer extreme pain.
Four more injections failed to have the desired effect, so Judith
decided she was going to have to shoot Lisa. As the girl pleaded for
her life, she led her to the canyon's edge and there shot her in the
back before pushing her over the ledge. She then changed her
jeans, leaving her blood-spattered pair at the scene.

The abduction of Janice Chatham had followed a similar pattern,
Judith said, although she'd had to shoot Janice three times because
the first two bullets had failed to kill her and she'd started
screaming.

With Judith's confession in hand, prosecutors must have thought
this would be a slam-dunk of a case. It was anything but. First
Robert French, Judith Neelley's court-appointed lawyer, filed a
petition to have the 18-year-old Judith tried as a minor. When that
was refused, he launched an insanity defense based on battered
woman syndrome. Judith admitted to shooting Lisa Ann and Janice
but said that she had done so only because she feared her husband
would kill her if she refused. Those who knew the couple thought
this unlikely. Judith, they said, was undoubtedly the dominant
partner.

In the end, French's efforts on behalf of his client were to no avail.
The case went to the jury on March 21, 1983, and they took less

than a day to return a verdict of guilty, with the recommendation of life in prison. Judge Cole, however, had other ideas. Ignoring the jury's recommendation, he sentenced Judith Ann Neelley to death.

Fearing a second death sentence, Judith then entered a guilty plea to the murder of Janice Chatman and drew a life sentence, plus ten years for the shooting of John Hancock. Alvin had meanwhile struck his own deal, drawing a life sentence for his part in the death of Janice Chatman.

At the age of just 18, Judith Ann Neelley was the youngest woman ever sentenced to death in the United States. She would remain incarcerated on Alabama's Death Row at the Julia Tutwiler Prison for Women until January 1999, when Alabama governor Fob James commuted her sentence to life in prison, just days before her execution. Neelley remains incarcerated in Alabama. Should she ever be paroled she will still have to serve out her life sentence in Tennessee.

Alvin Neelley served his sentence at Bostick State Prison in Tennessee. He died there in November 2005.

The Flowerpot Babies

Sabine Hilschenz

It is perhaps the most heinous crime of all, the murder of a child by its own mother. What then of a mother who murders nine of her offspring within minutes of birthing them? Just such a horrific case occurred in Frankfurt-on-Oder in the former East Germany between the years 1988 and 1999.

Sabine Hilschinz was born 1966 in Brieskow-Finkenheerd, East Germany, the daughter of a railway worker in the Communist state. A bright girl, with a recorded IQ of 120, Sabine excelled at school and went on to train as a dental hygienist. In her late teens, she caught the eye of police cadet Oliver Hilschinz. By the time they married, Oliver was upwardly mobile in the police force. He would eventually be recruited to the Stasi, the East German equivalent of Russia's KGB.

Life was good for the Hilschinzs in the early years of their marriage. Oliver's Stasi posting meant that they moved to the big city of Frankfurt. There, they produced three healthy children in the space of four years. Sabine gave up her job to care for her children. Not that she minded. She was a dedicated homemaker and a devoted mom. Things could hardly have been better.

But there were storm clouds gathering. East Germany, like most communist states of that era, was heading for economic meltdown. The government, in typical fashion, responded by cracking down, seeking to root out dissenters. It meant long periods away from home for Oliver Hilschinz, often amounting to weeks at a time. Alone, feeling abandoned and desperately lonely, Sabine started to look elsewhere for attention.

Sabine began visiting local taverns while Oliver was away and it wasn't long before she'd developed a drinking problem. She also began bringing home strangers for sex. As her drinking spiraled out of control and became alcoholism, she began neglecting her three children and they were taken into care by the state welfare services, but even that didn't stop her.

In October 1988, she became pregnant. Oliver, who was by now away constantly, barely noticed her condition, although on one occasion he did comment to Sabine that she was putting on weight. For her part, Sabine disguised her expanding belly by wearing wide, loose-fitting garments. She was worried, though, about what would happen after the baby was born. Oliver had made it clear that he did not want any more children.

One morning in May 1999, Sabine woke in great pain. Easing herself out of bed so as not to wake her sleeping husband, she waddled towards the bathroom, scooping up a vodka bottle on the way there. She sat down on the toilet seat and drank deeply from the bottle to ease her pain. As the contractions intensified, she bit down to silence her groans and continued taking long swigs from the vodka bottle. The baby, a girl, was born while Sabine sat on the toilet, its tiny head becoming immediately submerged in the bowl. Sabine made no effort to help the infant, allowing her to drown. She then cut the umbilical cord with a pair of scissors and carried the tiny corpse outside, where she buried it in a flowerpot on the balcony.

You would have thought that after such a horrific experience, Sabine Hilschinz would have given some thought to birth control. She didn't. Neither did she consider an abortion when she discovered she was pregnant again. The baby was carried to full term. After it was born, Sabine covered it with a blanket and left it to die. It too was buried in a flowerpot. A year later, she gave birth again, this time, discarding the baby's remains in a disused fish tank her husband kept in the garage.

Over the next decade, Sabine Hilschinz gave birth to six more children, all of them it would later be determined, fathered by her husband Oliver. During that period, neighbors noticed the growing number of flowerpots arrayed on the balcony of her Frankfurt apartment. Some contained flowers, others spring onions. They noticed too that Sabine enjoyed sitting on the balcony in the evening, talking in childlike tones, as though soothing an infant.

By 1999, Sabine and Oliver were separated and she decided to leave the apartment where she'd lived all of her married life. She decided to buy herself a camper van, the only problem being that the van was too small to hold all of her possessions. She found an easy solution for this, stashing most of her stuff in a garage at her mother's house. Sabine's mother, Eva, couldn't quite understand why Sabine would want to keep a broken down fish tank filled with earth, or why she wanted to store several flowerpots, but she didn't ask questions.

Sabine spent the next two years staying at various caravan parks in her camper van. Then, after her father died in 2001, her mother asked her to move into the family home. Sabine agreed and returned to the village of her birth. Shortly after she began dating an older man named Johann and became pregnant by him, giving birth to a healthy daughter.

Sabine Hilschinz's horrific crimes might have gone undetected indefinitely had her mother not decided to clear out the garage. Unable to carry out the heavy lifting herself, the elderly Eva asked a neighbor for help. "Keep whatever you want and throw out the rest," she told him.

The neighbor cast a skeptical eye over the pile of accumulated junk and then got to work. It wasn't long before he spotted something that he might be interested in keeping, a collection of rather attractive flowerpots. Picking up one of the pots he tipped it over and spilled the earth onto the garage floor. He got the shock of his life when a tiny human skeleton fell out.

The police would eventually find nine skeletons, some hidden in flowerpots, others in paint tins, one in the fish tank.

Sabine Hilschinz was arrested and charged with eight counts of manslaughter, the statute of limitations having expired on the first count. At trial, she offered an interesting defense, insisting that she wasn't sure whether the babies had been alive or stillborn. According to her, she'd been so drunk at the time of each birth that she'd passed out. The babies had been dead when she'd come to, she said.

The court disagreed, finding Sabine Hilschinz guilty of eight counts of manslaughter and sentencing her to 15 years in prison. Oliver Hilschinz was investigated as an accomplice but he was cleared. It seems that he genuinely didn't know that his wife had given birth to nine babies and killed them all.

My Mother Must Die

Tylar Witt was a typically rebellious teenager. A freshman at Oak Ridge High School, in El Dorado Hills, California, the pretty 14-year-old was into emo Goth style clothing, Japanese amine, and MySpace. She was often to be found hanging out at the Habit coffee shop in El Dorado, with a bunch of teens who shared similar interests.

Home life for Tylar was far from ideal. The only child of a single mother with whom she often clashed, Tylar had run away on several occasions. As a young child, she'd once been removed from her mother's custody, when Joanne Witt was still afflicted with a drinking problem. These days, Joanne had her demons under control, but she still struggled to control her rebellious daughter. For her part, Tylar had given up on running away. Her frustrations were channeled into inflicting self-harm with razor blades.

Around January 2009, Steven Colver, a 19-year-old who had recently graduated from Tylar's school, began hanging around at

Habits. He and Tylar struck up a friendship, Colver filling the "big brother" role, offering advice and guidance. They began talking regularly on the phone, with Tylar confiding the details of her difficult relationship with her mother. The platonic relationship evolved quickly and by March 2009, the two had slept together for the first time. Tylar was a virgin at the time and was instantly besotted, noting in her diary, "We will love each other past death. I know I will never stop loving him."

In April 2009, a series of events occurred that would serve to deepen the relationship between Colver and Witt and also set in motion a tragic chain of events. Steven Colver's father decided to move out of state, meaning Colver needed a place to stay. At the same time, Joanne Witt was looking to rent out a spare room in her house. Seizing on the opportunity, Tylar suggested to her mother that she rent the room to her friend, Steven. Joanne was at first hesitant to bring an older teenager into the home but eventually relented after Tylar told her that Steven was gay (Colver had, in fact, been involved in a gay relationship before meeting Tylar). Colver moved into the Witt home in April 2009, paying rent of $500 per month.

For the first few weeks, the arrangement worked wonderfully. The ultra-polite Colver helped with chores around the house and often interceded on Joanne's behalf when Tyler acted out. He even offered to tutor Tylar at math and e-mailed her teacher to get her assignments (Colver had aspirations of becoming a math teacher). To Joanne, Steven Colver must have seemed like a godsend. She, of course, didn't see the stolen kisses, much less what went on when she was out of the house. It took only six weeks before the illusion was shattered.

On May 13, 2009, Joanne found a bottle of sexual lubricant, various sex toys and a stash of marijuana in the house. Not wanting to believe that the objects belonged to Tylar, she confronted Steven. He readily admitted that the stash was his, but insisted that he was only holding it for a friend. He was calm and unerringly polite and Joanne was convinced. He initial instinct had been to ask him to move out, but she decided to let him stay. It was a move she'd come to regret almost immediately.

Just the next day, Joanne returned home unexpectedly. Not finding Tylar in her room she walked down the hall to Colver's bedroom, intending to ask him if he knew where Tylar was. When she knocked on the door, she heard scurried movement. Colver didn't open the door for several minutes. When he did, he was wearing only his jeans. Sensing something amiss, Joanne pushed into the room and opened the closet, where she found Tylar naked, save for a yellow sports bra that she held clutched to her chest.

Joanne was shocked to discover that her 14-year-old daughter was having sex with her 19-year-old boarder. She spent the rest of the afternoon mulling over how to deal with the situation. Eventually, she asked Colver to take a drive with her to a local park where the two of them could talk things over. There, a contrite Colver admitted that he and Tylar had been sleeping together for over two months. Anxious to keep the matter out of the public eye, Joanne agreed not to press charges of statutory rape, provided Colver moved out of the house immediately and stopped seeing Tylar. He agreed.

☐ ☐ ☐

A few days after Stephen Colver moved out of the Witt home, Joanne had cause to go back on her word, when Tylar went missing. Convinced that she was with Colver, Joanne called the police and filed rape charges. Tylar, as it turned out, was with a female friend, not with Colver, but the damage was done. The police hauled the pair in for questioning about their relationship. They told a similar story, insisting that they were friends and nothing more. The incident where Joanne had found Tylar naked in Colver's room had been a misunderstanding, they said. Tylar had been there modeling clothes for Colver, not engaging in sex. Colver was, in fact, gay. Unable to break either of them under interrogation, the police were forced to let the matter drop.

The rape allegations served to further erode the relationship between Joanne Witt and her daughter. Tylar was angry at her mother for trying to have Colver charged with a criminal act. For her part, Joanne remained committed to exposing the truth about Colver's illicit relationship with Tylar. She found it in Tylar's diary, described in graphic detail. Also in the diary, Tylar opened up about her feelings towards her mother, including elaborate fantasies about Joanne dying in a car accident.

Those entries, the one's describing Tylar's feeling towards her, left Joanne in a quandary. She now had the evidence to put Steven Colver away, but she didn't want the police to read about her personal relationship with her daughter. She decided to have the police speak to Tylar one more time, to see if they could convince her to come clean about her sexual relationship with Colver. However, when El Dorado Sheriff's Deputy Ken Barber called on the Witt home on June 10, Tylar's stuck to her story. Joanne then gave Barber the diary.

Tylar was outraged when she heard that her mother had handed her diary over to the police. On the evening of June 11, 2009, she and Colver exchanged several phone calls. Then, around midnight, with Joanne having retired to bed, Colver showed up at the house. Sometime before daybreak on June 12, the lovers left the house together. They planned on traveling to San Francisco, where they would commit suicide together in an ending worthy of Romeo and Juliet. First, though, they were going to spend the day in El Dorado Hills, saying goodbye to friends.

Joanne Witt did not show up for work on Friday, June 12, but her colleagues were not overly concerned. Joanne had skipped work before, usually when she had to deal with some crisis of her daughter's making. However, when she still hadn't shown on Monday, June 15, they reported the matter to the police and asked them to check on Joanne. When officers found the house locked and no one responding to the doorbell, Joanne's father, Norbert Witt, was called. He arrived to allow the officers in. They were unprepared for what they found.

Joanne Witt lay on her bed, in a pool of congealed blood, a gore-soaked Spongebob Squarepants blanket drawn over her. An autopsy would later reveal that she'd been stabbed 20 times in the neck and chest.

Steven Colver and Tylar Witt, meanwhile, had checked into a Holiday Inn in downtown San Francisco. They'd spent the weekend sightseeing, doing drugs and writing suicide notes, which they mailed to Matt Widman, Colver's friend and former lover. They then made a halfhearted attempt to follow through on their suicide pact. First, they tried ingesting rat poison, but couldn't bring themselves to eat enough of the substance to cause actual harm. Next, they tried cutting their wrists, but Colver couldn't bear to inflict pain on himself. Finally, Colver suggested jumping off the hotel's roof, but Tylar said she couldn't do it, as she was afraid of heights.

Aware by now that the police were probably looking for them, Colver and Witt decided to head south, leaving San Francisco on foot on June 16. The following morning, they were spotted by a police officer in the town of San Bruno and placed under arrest.

□ □ □ □

From the outset, it was decided that Tylar Witt would be tried as an adult. The evidence against both of the defendants was pretty solid and a long prison term surely awaited. However, Witt's attorney was able to strike a deal. She'd testify against Colver in exchange for a reduced charge of second-degree murder and parole eligibility in 15 years. With that deal in place, prosecutors were confident that a conviction against Colver was a mere formality. It didn't turn out that way.

The Colver / Witt trial soon descended into a case of he said / she said. According to Tylar, Colver had planned the murder and wielded the knife. But Colver told a different story. He said that he'd arrived at the Witt residence to find Joanne Witt already dead and Tylar holding a bloody knife. All he was guilty of was covering up the crime.

In the end, it was up to the jury to decide and they came down on the side of Tylar Witt. Steven Colver was found guilty of first-degree murder with aggravating circumstances and was sentenced to a term of life in prison without the possibility of parole. Tylar Witt was found guilty of second-degree murder. Her sentence was 15 years to life.

Robert Keller

Hear No Evil

It seemed the most unlikely place for a killer to be lurking, a renowned learning institution for the deaf and hearing impaired, which had been inaugurated by Abraham Lincoln in 1864. And yet, between September 2000 and February 2001, just such a person haunted the hallowed halls of Washington DC's Gallaudet University.

At around 8:00 pm on September 28, 2000, Gallaudet student Joseph Mesa Jr. approached resident advisor Thomas Koch to complain about a vile odor emanating from one of the dorm rooms in Cogswell Hall. The room belonged to 19-year-old Eric Plunkett, a student from Minnesota. Plunkett hadn't been seen all day, Mesa said. His friends were worried about him.

Knowing that Eric Plunkett suffered from cerebral palsy and concerned that he might have suffered a fall, Koch went to check on him. He detected none of the foul odor Mesa had told him about but decided to enter the room anyway, using a passkey. Inside it was dark, so Koch turned on a light and immediately spotted Eric lying on the floor. Eric wasn't breathing and the severe bruising to his face suggested that he'd been severely beaten. Koch went immediately to notify school officials.

It wasn't long before Cogswell Hall was swarming with uniformed cops and crime scene investigators. As they began processing the scene, it became evident that someone inside the university, a student or faculty member, had bludgeoned Eric Plunkett to death, the murder weapon most probably a chair found in the room. Given the tight security on the campus, it was unlikely that an outsider could have gotten in and out unnoticed. Detectives, therefore, focused their attention on finding anyone who might have had an altercation with Plunkett. They soon had a suspect.

Thomas Minch, 18, had come to Gallaudet from Greenland, New Hampshire. He and Eric were close and Thomas had been hard hit by his friend's murder. He had helped arrange a memorial service for Eric and had even posted a eulogy to Eric on his Web page. However, all had not been well between the friends. Another student told police about a fight between the two of them shortly before Eric's death.

Questioned about the incident, Minch readily admitted that he and Eric had quarreled. He even admitted that the altercation had become physical and that he'd struck Eric. At that point, the officers ended the interview and charged Thomas Minch with second-degree murder.

The arrest did not hold for long. At the arraignment, the U.S. Attorney's office dropped the charges against Minch, citing insufficient evidence. However, the detective heading up the case still believed that Minch was his man and continued to seek evidence against him. In the meantime, Minch was suspended from Gallaudet, and returned home, his dreams of a higher education in tatters. He was back in DC, along with his parents and attorney, in February 2001, to attend a grand jury. Those proceedings had barely started before it was clear that Thomas Minch had not killed Eric Plunkett.

In the early morning hours of February 3, 2001, a fire alarm sounded on the fourth floor at Cogswell Hall. The resident advisor who went to investigate the commotion noticed that the door to one of the dorm rooms stood open. He went to investigate and immediately spotted the blood-spattered body of 19-year-old Benjamin Varner, lying on the floor.

For the second time in just over three months, homicide investigators were summoned to Cogswell Hall. An autopsy would later reveal that Benjamin had been stabbed multiple times in his head, chest, and neck. One of his lungs had collapsed, and his throat had been slashed. Such was the ferocity of the attack that the knife had penetrated his skull in at least one place.

The police soon picked up a few promising clues, including the imprint of a Nike cross-trainer in Benjamin's blood, and a bloodstained jacket and knife in a trash can just outside the dormitory. What they didn't have was a suspect. Evidence suggested that Benjamin had been murdered the previous day and it seemed obvious that whoever had triggered the alarm had done so in order that his body would be discovered. The question was, who had triggered the alarm? Nobody knew, or at least, nobody was admitting to it.

With fears that a serial killer might be stalking the Gallaudet students, the FBI was called into the investigation and a $10,000 reward was offered for information leading to an arrest. Meanwhile, the university beefed up security, implemented identity checks on anyone entering campus and installed surveillance cameras. Cogswell Hall itself was closed and students were reassigned to other dorms. Despite these measures, a number of students left the university, fearful for their safety.

As the police investigation continued, detectives followed several lines of inquiry and one of them paid dividends. It emerged that Benjamin's checkbook had been stolen, so the police looked into his financial transactions. They quickly picked up something amiss. On Friday, February 2, someone had cashed one of Benjamin's checks at a branch of Riggs Bank. Knowing that it could not have been Benjamin, the police requested video surveillance footage from the bank. It showed a young man with dark hair completing the transaction. The check, it emerged, was made out to a Gallaudet student, and Cogswell Hall resident, named Joseph Mesa. The same Joseph Mesa who had complained about the stench coming from Eric Plunkett's room.

When police brought Mesa in for questioning they knew immediately that he was the man on the video. Then, after Secret Service handwriting experts confirmed that it was Mesa and not Benjamin Varner who had written the check, Mesa was arrested and charged with murder.

Twenty-year-old Joseph Mesa was a freshman at Gallaudet. He was originally from Guam and had been friendly with both victims. Looking into his background, detectives discovered a disturbing pattern of behavior. Although pleasant and friendly, Mesa was a habitual thief. Other students spoke of seeing him stealing money and he'd once stolen a debit card from his roommate and used it to the extent of several thousand dollars. That had earned him a suspension from the university but he'd been allowed to return. Now he stood accused of two counts of murder.

Communicating through an interpreter, Mesa initially denied murder. However, after several interviews, he eventually cracked and admitted to the crimes. "To be honest with you," he told detectives, "I did it."

He then went on to describe how he'd killed Benjamin Varner. The motive had been money, he said. He'd gone to Benjamin's room specifically to rob him. Arriving at around 9:00 pm on the night of February 1, he'd asked Benjamin if he had a checkbook. When Benjamin said that he did, Mesa had picked up a knife from a counter and stabbed him in the back of the neck. When Benjamin fell to the floor, Mesa had straddled him and slit his throat. He then took the checkbook and made out a check to himself for $650, after which he fled the room, leaving in such a hurry that he'd forgotten to take the murder weapon with him. He'd later returned to retrieve the knife and had dumped it in a bin on the campus, together with his bloodied clothes. Pressed on the murder of Eric Plunkett, Mesa again admitted that he was the killer and that the motive had again been robbery. He said that he'd chosen the two victims because he thought they'd be easy to overpower.

Mesa's story was inconsistent with the facts. Specifically, it failed to mention the nineteen knife wounds inflicted on Benjamin Varner. Nonetheless, the police decided not to pressure Mesa on the issue. They were certain that they'd captured the Cogswell Hall killer.

Based on the confession, the police obtained a warrant to search Mesa's new residence, in the adjacent Krug Hall. There they found a pair of bloody Nikes that matched the footprint left at the scene. They also found bloodstained clothing and credit cards belonging to the two victims.

Joseph Mesa's trial was set for November 2001 and the case looked about as clear-cut as it could get. But even as attorneys on both sides waited to bring the matter to trial, stories began to appear in the Washington Post of a botched police investigation. According to the reports, Joseph Mesa should have immediately been a suspect in the Eric Plunkett murder. Mesa had taken Eric's wallet from the scene and had used his credit card on the day of his death, although the police failed to follow this up. Mesa should also have been considered the number one suspect, as it was he who'd drawn attention to the murder. This was standard police procedure but they'd failed to follow it, choosing to focus instead on Thomas Minch.

Had the police looked into Mesa's background they would have discovered his suspension from the university for theft. That should have caused them to focus their attention on Mesa and would quite possibly have prevented the second murder. The police had been negligent and Assistant Police Chief Terrance W.

Gainer admitted as much. "We are accountable," he told the Post. "We need to do better." It was scant consolation for the grieving families of the victims, or for the wrongly accused Thomas Minch.

After several legal delays, Joseph Mesa eventually went on trial on February 19, 2002. His legal team initially tried an insanity defense, claiming that their client suffered from a condition known as "Intermittent Explosive Disorder" which rendered him incapable of controlling his violent impulses. However, Mesa's videotaped confession, detailing as it did the planning that went into the murders, contradicted this. Mesa then tried another tack. He said that he was ordered to kill by voices. Only, in his case, it was not words but a pair of gloved hands that appeared to him in visions and gave commands to kill in sign language.

This story was given short shrift by the jury. In the end, they took just three hours to convict Mesa on two counts of first-degree murder. Joseph Mesa was sentenced to life in prison without the possibility of parole.

After the conclusion of the trial Thomas Minch was offered the opportunity to return to Gallaudet, but declined. He has since filed a lawsuit for wrongful arrest and defamation of character. Cogswell Hall was shut down as a dorm and converted into a general use building. A memorial at the entrance pays tribute to Eric Plunkett and Benjamin Varner.

For more True Crime books by Robert Keller please visit

http://bit.ly/kellerbooks

17165481R00068

Printed in Great Britain
by Amazon